OLD HERBACEOUS

Reginald Arkell

Old Herbaceous

HARCOURT, BRACE AND COMPANY

New York

COPYRIGHT, 1951, BY
HARCOURT, BRACE AND COMPANY, INC.

*All rights reserved, including
the right to reproduce this book
or portions thereof in any form.*

first American edition

PRINTED IN THE UNITED STATES OF AMERICA

The mists be on the river bed,
    The roses all be gone;
And here be I, about to die,
    With Harvest coming on.
Dear Lord, I've traipsed some weary miles,
I'll be main glad to rest awhiles.

The folk'll soon be in the fields
    A-getting in the grain;
For most of those, the time You've chose
    Be awkerd in the main.
Though not so bad, 'tis sure, for they
As be a-workin' by the day.

September be a better month
    For all the carter men;
And when I die don't signify,
    So let I bide till then:
The wagons'll be standing by,
And there'll be time to bury I.

              (from *Green Fingers Again*)

OLD HERBACEOUS

CHAPTER ONE

It was one of those mild autumn mornings when early mist had turned to soft rain and water dripped from everything. No real touch of winter yet; just a soft pause between the seasons, giving you the best of both. Not too warm, as it had been; not too cold, as it would be. . . .

This was the time of year and the time of day that the old man loved best. He couldn't get around so much now, but they had made up his bed by the cottage window, and there he would sit, half waking and half sleeping, dreaming of this and that.

From where he sat, propped up among his cushions, he could see into the Manor gardens. Not what they were—not by a long chalk. . . . Mind you, it was only fair to admit they were still a bit short-handed, and you had to take the dry summer into account, but these young fellows ought to have made a better job of it than that. . . . When he was a young chap, he had to move at double their pace. No slipping off when the clock struck for him. Hours he'd spent watering when the sun was off the borders. . . . But not today. That meant overtime, and where was the money to pay for that? So the old garden wasn't what it had been when he was in charge.

Everything was different to what it was in his day. They earned more money, and that was only right. But the more they got, the less they seemed to care. You had to be proud of a garden to do any good with it. Gardening was a whole-time job, like the cows or the sheep. Cows had to be milked, whatever happened; and who thought of stopping in bed when the sheep were lambing? In a garden, you had to work with the seasons. There were slack times, when you could take an easy with a pipe behind the tool shed, but when the grass started growing and the weeds were getting on top of you, there was an end to all that nonsense. . . . Hours he'd spent watering. . . . But these young fellows. . . .

That was the trouble nowadays. Nobody seemed to care any more. When he was a boy, you'd see the farm chaps and their families walking round in their Sunday clothes as though the place belonged to them. Showing off, they were. Proud of the work they'd done during the week. Laughing at young Harry's crooked furrows. Scuffling up a bit of spring wheat to see how it was doing. Cowman bragging to his missus about his herd. Shepherd making sure there wasn't a sheep on its back. . . . Then, if the farmer came along, they'd all have a friendly chat and everyone would learn something. . . . Good days, those were. . . . Good days.

Same with the garden. When he was in charge across the way, he never felt that he was just a paid man working for a wage. He felt that the place was his—and so it was, in a manner of speaking. He learned that from old John Addis, his first head gardener. Very quiet, old John was—very quiet and respectful, up to a point; but when it came to an argy-bargy with the young missus, there was no doubt who was boss. "Very well, Addis," she would say, "if you think that's how it should be done, I've no objection." And when it came to picking flowers for the house, they always had to ask old John about it. . . . But not today. . . . Anyone could pick anything, because nobody cared any more. . . .

Looking out of his little window, the old man saw that the early morning mist had cleared, as though a gauze curtain had been raised to reveal the bright detail of a theatrical scene. The dahlias, not yet blackened by the first frost; Michaelmas daisies and petunias, still making splashes of color against a gray wall; the berries of a cotoneaster looking like a regiment of toy soldiers in ceremonial uniform. . . .

In the shrubberies, the yellowing nut bushes gave the first hint of autumn's final golden cavalcade. Very soon, the flowering shrubs would add their reds and oranges to the picture; coral berries would glisten behind the gothic foliage of the spindle trees and the great leaves of the catalpa would trace their crazy pattern on the wet grass. There would be the final flurry of butterflies round the last bit of buddleia. . . .

Truly a gracious and very English scene, as he had known it for more than three-quarters of a century. People said that big gardens were finished; that everything belonged to everybody and nothing to anybody. He didn't believe that. The world started with a garden and a thing that had been going all that time wouldn't end so easily. Anyway, they would last out his time and what happened after he'd gone wasn't his business.

Gardens! The old man closed his eyes and let his thoughts wander through the scented past. A long journey, up-hill most of the way, but it had led somewhere, and no mistake. . . . Started as a nobody and ended as a somebody. . . . That day when he was asked to judge at the County Show. . . . Lunch in the big marquee, and him sitting up at the top table. . . . Those were the days. . . . A young fellow could push his way through and rise to anything. . . . If he wasn't afraid of work and took an interest in his job.

Well, he'd stuck to it, and he'd come out at the top. Respected, he was. They might laugh at him behind his back, some of the young ones. Called him "Old Herbaceous" when they thought he wasn't listening. But they never took liberties. After all, he was a bit of a perennial. . . . Eighty years he'd been going. . . . So let them have their little joke. . . .

That was the best of growing old. You didn't get hot under the collar about little things and you didn't have to worry about the future. . . . Time was too short for that. . . . Here he was, living in his own cottage and enough in the Post Office to see him through. . . . Anything he had he could pay for. . . . He wasn't dependent on one of them. . . . What they did for him they got paid for, and very glad they were to find the money on the corner of the mantelpiece every Saturday morning. . . .

That was the right way for a man to finish, and that was how it was going to be. . . .

CHAPTER TWO

On a certain Thursday in November 1789 was effected what the *Morning Post* described as "the greatest object of internal Navigation in this Kingdom." The Severn was united to the Thames by an intermediate canal, ascending to the height of 343 feet, by 40 locks; there entering a tunnel through the hill of Saperton, for the length of two miles and three furlongs, and descending by 27 locks to join the Thames near Lechlade.

When the first boat completed this tremendous journey, she was welcomed by vast crowds who answered a salute of twelve pieces of cannon by loud huzzas. A dinner was given at five of the principal Inns, and the day ended with ringing of bells, a bonfire and a ball.

"With respect to the internal commerce of the Kingdom and the security of communication in time of war," concluded the *Morning Post*, "this junction of the Thames and Severn must, for all time, be attended with the most beneficial consequences."

So much for the vanity of human prognostications. Within fifty years the railways had sealed the fate of inland water transport, and, in another fifty, the Thames and Severn canal was as near derelict as made no difference. . . .

But no depressing reflections on mutability and decay troubled the minds of the small country boys who, in the 'seventies, perched on the hump-backed bridge and exchanged dubious courtesies with the ageing lock-keeper who lived in the curious little Roundhouse. His job was almost a sinecure, for though the canal was still officially navigable, a week might pass before the next barge came through. And then it would only bring a load of coal for the villages or pick up sacks of barley sold by some local farmer to the brewers at Bristol.

So the lock-keeper, a contraptious old buffer, if ever there was one, had time enough to battle with his young tormentors and the canal settled down to the nostalgic task of forgetting its former glories.

Among the urchins who picked stones from the bridge and threw them into the stagnant water was one who did not enter largely into the spirit of the thing. Like his companions, he wore the discarded corduroys and hobnailed boots of his seniors, but his features had a finer line, and one of his scraggy little legs was a shade shorter than the other; the result of rough horse-play in which he had had the worst of the bargain. His "back answers" to the contraptious old buffer lacked the snap of his fellows; possibly because he couldn't run as fast as they could; and even when the occasional barge crawled round the corner of the canal, he was more concerned with the yellow flags and ragged robins that, each year, encroached more and more upon this dwindling waterway.

At this point in his ruminations, Old Herbaceous stirred uneasily among his cushions. He loved wandering in the past, especially along the banks of the old canal, but always the picture of himself, so different from the other boys, came as a disturbing element. For different he had certainly been and for a very good reason.

Opening her cottage door, on a May morning some eighty-odd years ago, Mrs. Pinnegar, the cowman's wife, had received a shock, and no mistake. There, on the doorstep, wrapped in an old cotton skirt, was a baby, as newly-born as made no difference. Mrs. Pinnegar, a kindly soul, with six children of her own, passed the village maidens in review. Several of them were "expecting," but Mrs. Pinnegar, unofficial midwife and friend of all families, knew their dates to a nicety and the problem was not so easily solved. There had been no gypsies through the village for weeks. . . . Being a practical woman, the cowman's wife picked up the parcel the fairies had brought her; christened it Herbert, after an uncle who was killed in the Crimea, and set about her Monday's wash. When you had six of your own, one more didn't matter.

Naturally, there was a bit of chatter at the time, but unexpected arrivals never made front-page news in an English village. A rick fire and talk of the Prussians in Paris were much more exciting. Young Herbert settled down in his new home; seasons came and went; the new self-binder started tying the sheaves with string. . . .

Still, being picked up on a door-step did take the gilt off the gingerbread a bit; especially when you'd got along in the world and become someone in the village. True, there was nobody left to throw his birth in his teeth. Everybody was dead—every man Jack of them! Old folk went and new folk came, until you couldn't find a single soul who remembered anything. Very soon he'd go, too, and then there'd be nothing left but houses—and gardens.

Funny, that! You planted a tree; you watched it grow; you picked the fruit and, when you were old, you sat in the shade of it. Then you died and they forgot all about you—just as though you had never been. . . . But the tree went on growing, and everybody took it for granted. It always had been there and it always would be there. . . . Everybody ought to plant a tree, sometime or another—if only to keep them humble in the sight of the Lord.

Old Herbaceous wasn't what you would call a religious man. Only when deeply moved would he bring his Creator into it. These occasions were infrequent and were usually concerned with husbandry. The spiritual welfare of a human being was the parson's concern, but a tree suffering from elm disease was a different kettle of fish. . . . On such occasions the First Gardener was called in to give a second opinion, and what He said usually went.

This rather primitive unorthodoxy had worried a succession of incumbents up at the old Vicarage. Each succeeding padre had angled artfully for the soul of this errant parishioner, without any conspicuous success. Several of them had been aware of religious convictions tucked away somewhere, but not one had secured an out-and-out conversion. Very baffling! Hurrying down to his three-hour service, an earnest young priest had stopped to ask the old man if he knew what Good Friday was all about. "Good Friday?" came the reply. "Good Friday be the day when the Almighty reckons we ought to get our 'taties in."

Actually, this question of religion had bothered Old Herbaceous more than a bit during his eighty-year traffic with earthly things. Whenever he had called the Almighty into conference, he had done so with an unswerving faith that he was talking to an equal whose advice could be relied upon in an emergency. But what *was* an emergency? He couldn't be forever tapping at the golden gates, as you might say. After all, he was only one of millions. And so was born an increasing diffidence which threatened a very pleasant relationship with almost total extinction. As though you were forever asking favors of a friend and suddenly realized that you might be overdoing it.

Now and again, of course, you could make a bit of a splash, just to show how you felt about things. When old Mrs. Pinnegar died, for instance, he had given her a funeral such as had never been seen in the village. Stripped the greenhouse, he had, till there wasn't a flower left. That was one for the old lady—and one for the Almighty. He could see her coffin now; or, rather, he couldn't see it for lilies, carnations, orchids. He'd felt easier in his mind after that, but he still owed both of them something, and he wouldn't forget to let them know it when his time came. . . .

Having thus set his mind at rest, the old man let his thoughts wander back more happily to the hump-backed bridge over the old canal, and the small boy in the torn corduroys and hob-nailed boots. He was always happier thinking of those days. He could remember people better.

See their faces and hear their voices. Like History. There was a lot in the middle that didn't seem to mean much, but ask him about Alfred the Great or William the Conqueror and he had no trouble at all.

He remembered, as if it was yesterday, the first day he went to the village school. It was presided over by a large, comfortable lady who frightened the life out of everybody—including the vicar, who was chairman of the Governors and came in on Wednesdays to take the weekly scripture lesson.

Mary Brain was her name, a robust person with a robust appearance, who employed robust methods to secure her inevitable goal. There was no unnecessary finesse about her. She did not move in a mysterious way her wonders to perform. Not she! She knew exactly where she was going and you either got out of her way or you were trampled to death. A human steam roller with a very good sense of direction. The sort of all-round woman who, we like to say, is not born nowadays. Which is, of course, all nonsense.

She had never married, and the reason was once put to her by a rather impudent young undergraduate who punted up from Oxford to discover the real source of the Thames. Mary Brain, a much younger and slimmer person then, was down in the meadow looking for the first snake's-head fritillary. They sat and talked, through a long summer evening, but when he tried to kiss her, she sent him about his business—which was, of course, to discover the true source of the Thames.

Outraged pride made the young man eloquent. "The trouble with you," he told her, "is that you look so darned efficient, so capable, so competent. Positively frightening! Why do you wear those awful spectacles?"

"Because I'm short-sighted."

"That's no reason. No girl with nice eyes should wear spectacles. Take them off. Throw them in the river. Go on, throw them in the river!"

Under the spell of this dynamic young man, Mary Brain removed her spectacles; closed them carefully and —threw them into the river. But her preceptor in the art of fascination was not satisfied.

"And now your hair," he remarked, briskly. "Much too sensible."

"What must I do with my hair," asked Mary, mildly, "throw it in the river?"

There was a dangerous gleam in the young man's eye. "I'll show you what to do with your hair," he said.

And there, on the banks of the silver Isis, he ruffled her severely braided tresses, until she looked as though she had been dragged through a hedge, backwards. Then he stood back and considered his handiwork.

What he saw seemed to satisfy him.

"Much better," he said. "That's taken some of the starch out of you. Keep it up! I'll be back one of these days."

A vigorous stroke of the paddle took him round the corner, and he was gone.

CHAPTER THREE

Mary Brain went back to her school-house. She bought herself a new pair of spectacles and settled down to be more kindly and more competent than ever. She never married, but every now and again it was remarked that her hair was a bit wild like, as though someone had run their fingers through it.

Having no children of her own, she dealt faithfully with those in her charge; and every now and again one would come in for special mothering. This wouldn't be, necessarily, the brightest scholar or the lamest duck. Two blue eyes would smile shyly from the third row and all Mary's defenses would come down with a crash. Thereafter, the bewildered infant found himself possessed of a second home and a second mother, which usually functioned more comfortably than those to which he rightly belonged.

So it was that young Herbert, creeping like a frightened kitten into a strange, cold world, discovered a wonderful new heaven where he really meant something to somebody at last. Sometimes, in the past, Mary's maternal instincts had caused jealousies and talk of favoritism, but, as nobody bothered about what happened to a motherless brat after school hours, no serpent reared its head in this particular Eden.

Almost any summer evening, these two would be seen walking along the towpath of the old canal. Sometimes they would stop to pick some wild flower that took their fancy and then they would talk earnestly about its special features. Sometimes they would pull it to pieces and hold a sort of inquest upon it. Mary Brain was the greatest authority on wild flowers in the county; so that, of young Herbert it began to be said that "what he didn't know about wild flowers wasn't worth knowing."

The old canal was their favorite hunting-ground for two reasons. In the first place, you could walk along it without having some angry farmer shouting at you. Farmers, in those days, were real dogs in the manger. They had no use for wild flowers—hated them in fact—but they wouldn't let anyone else enjoy them. If you so much as picked a moon daisy in the corner of a field of mowing grass they made as much fuss as though you had set fire to a rick. No doubt they were pestered by poachers and trespassers, but they might have a bit of sense.

After one or two such encounters, young Herbert began to hate and detest all farmers. It hurt his pride to be shouted at across a ten-acre field for picking an early primrose. To him, all weeds were flowers, while to the farmer all flowers were weeds, so there was little hope of an understanding. Never, never, he promised himself, would he go on a farm when he left school. He would rather get a job scraping the side of the road, or being an odd-job man, or—or anything. No farming for him; not if he knew it!

The second thing to be said for the old canal was its wonderful richness in plant life. Even as long ago as that, the occasional barge had to push its way between borders of yellow flags, water bubbles, wild heliotrope and a dozen other exuberant growths. If you took half a step, the smell of water mint under your feet almost knocked you over; ragged robins had a style and color all their own and as for the wild forget-me-nots. . . .

Sometimes young Herbert would put a real poser to his companion. Which wild flower did she like best? He had no doubts on the subject, but he wanted to hear his choice endorsed by higher authority. Having asked his question he would hug himself in delightful anticipation, for *he* knew, and *she* knew that there was nothing to touch wild forget-me-nots. Those you grew in a garden weren't a patch on them. When he had a garden of his own, he would dig a hole, fill it with water and plant wild forget-me-nots all round it.

It was their color that bowled him over. There never was such a blue and there never would be. Young Herbert hadn't seen a gentian, nor even the lovely *Ipomoea Nemophila Leari,* but with the easy confidence of youth he was prepared to back his own opinion. The time would come when he would change his opinion, but grudgingly, and with many nostalgic apologies to the old canal and its wild forget-me-nots.

Apart from the flowers, the wild life of the countryside did not interest him at all. Birds' eggs, perhaps, but only to look at. One day he found a strange nest in the middle of a thorn bush. He couldn't get up to it, so he got a crooked stick and pulled down a corner. It was full of young birds and one of them fell out. Young Herbert buried the naked little fledgling and felt awful about it. That cured him of birds'-nesting.

Terrified as he was of farmers, young Herbert didn't have to bother when sailing in convoy, as you might say. Mary Brain would cruise through enemy waters, like a privateer of old, with all sails set and a broadside of guns stripped ready for action. Heaven help the unlucky farmer who interfered with her on her unlawful occasions. Young Herbert's knees would knock together like a couple of castanets, even though he knew they would come out of the engagement with flying colors. To do the farmers justice, they did not go about looking for trouble. Peaceful men, they put their telescopes to their blind eyes and held their fire for a more suitable occasion.

So the two malefactors ranged the countryside, seeking adventures strange and new. Sometimes it was a wild orchis of a quite unfamiliar species; at others it would be a sinister henbane drooping its viscous wings on a discarded rubbish heap. And as they rambled happily together, like a couple of old cronies, the teacher packed the pupil's receptive mind with the store of facts which stood him in such good stead when the days of his apprenticeship were over.

All of which might suggest that young Herbert was developing into a bit of a mollycoddle; what with his bad foot, and always being tied to teacher's apron strings. One or two little toughs, laboring under this delusion, thought it was safe to have a bit of a game with him. So they got a girl's apron and started to put it round him. They didn't try again. For the only time in his life, young Herbert developed a cold fury which frightened the lives out of them. There was no kicking or throwing stones. Just a very small boy with a very white face; so bitterly scornful that, suddenly, all the fun went out of the game. Groping back into his dubious parentage, young Herbert had found a champion and developed a personality. Perhaps there was some advantage in being nobody's child, after all.

This rather odd kink came out in all sorts of ways. Skating on the canal, for instance. In those days, skating was not a poor man's game. It wasn't the actual cost of the skates, so much as a sense of fitness which kept the upper and the lower classes from performing on the same pond. Quite calmly and without any fuss, young Herbert cut through all such social conventions. He got hold of a pair of old skates; corrected his lameness by fixing a bit of wood to the sole of his left boot and taught himself all the tricks of balance and speed inside half an hour. Once he was on the ice he was a transformed being. Something gave him wings and the limping little boy became a swallow in flight.

And here was where the old canal once again played its part. When the frost started, skating was confined to the floods in the meadows, but, as it continued, the ice on the canal bore and, if it hadn't been for the locks, you could have skated from Thames to Severn without stopping. The water under the little hump-backed bridges was the last to freeze, and careful souls left the ice and hobbled to the farther side of the bridge until some more daring spirit blazed the trail.

Young Herbert was always first under the bridges. Working up a high speed, he would put his feet together and let his momentum carry him safely through. This was pioneering of a rather high order, calling for skill, judgment and courage, for the smallest error in timing would have landed him under the ice with no hope of escape. Old-timers, with memories of former accidents, held their breath, but the small boy made no mistakes and his career during the months of the Big Freeze became a legend in the villages.

Success in any field is a stimulating thing. Young Herbert came out of that hard winter strengthened and comforted. By the time the ice melted, it was a very different small boy who unscrewed his old skates and threw away the bit of wood that, for a month or two, had made him the equal in stature of his fellows. He knew now that, given the opportunity, he was as good as the best of them. If a bit of wood on the sole of your shoe made all that difference, he had nothing to worry about. What he could do on the ice he could do anywhere.

As for those other boys, farmers' sons who had new clothes every year and went to the Grammar School, he wasn't afraid of them any more. He had seen them watching him, wishing they could skate as well as he could, afraid to be first under the bridges! Well, if there was a good frost next winter, he'd show them a few more tricks.

From which it will be seen that young Herbert was shedding his inferiority complex as a snake sheds its skin in the spring sunshine. And it never came back—not really; though now and again, Old Herbaceous, dozing among his cushions, would still feel a twinge of the old enemy.

After all, it *was* a bit of a pill, coming into the world as nobody's child, though even that drawback seemed to have a sort of advantage in making you different in a kind of way. If he'd been just one of the village boys, he'd have gone on the farm and pushed a plow for the rest of his life. Never sat at the same table as a real, live lord and talked to him as man to man. Never been a proper gardener. . . .

Funny how things worked out. You never knew what was best for you in the long run and it was the long run that mattered. Looking at him now, some of these young fellows might think he hadn't traveled very far, but they should have seen him in the hour of his glory.

A shaft of sunlight slid through a pane of the cottage window, lighting up a gold challenge cup, until it shone like an oriflamme. Old Herbaceous smiled happily. Yes, these young fellows should have seen him in the hour of his glory. . . .

CHAPTER FOUR

When, a week before the Annual Flower Show, young Herbert announced that he would enter for the wild flower competition, Mary Brain gave him a syllabus, with her blessing, and turned him out of the cottage, with instructions not to come back until the show was over.

She knew, none better, how village tongues wagged, especially when you won a prize at the show. Two things brought out all that was worst in their little community: decorating the church for Easter or Christmas, when jealousies were rampant; and winning a prize at the flower show, when the most appalling slanders were launched about the successful competitors.

If by some odd chance young Herbert *should* catch the Judges' eye, everyone would say she had helped him with selection and arrangement of his exhibit, just as they always said Dan'l Green never could grow carrots and Silas Mustoe had borrowed a couple of parsnips from the head gardener at the Big House. All of which she explained to the budding champion before closing the door and sending him about his business.

Thus turned adrift, young Herbert tasted the bittersweets of personal responsibility for the first time. Once again he felt like the kitten that gets the sharp end of its mother's claw and is told to catch mice for itself in future. Now he would have to draw on his own personal store of experience and moral courage. Even though he knew where to find flowers and what to call them, he still had to face those fearful farmers who appeared suddenly from nowhere and bellowed at you, like the big bull they sometimes led along the road with a ring in its nose.

So terrifying was this prospect that young Herbert very nearly called it a day. Until he thought of the old canal where flowers grew like weeds and nobody minded how many you picked. He would lose a lot by not venturing into the fields, but a queer instinct told him that something was to be gained by specializing. Besides, most of the flowers he really liked grew by the canal, and, as they grew together, so they would look well together. Like people who had always known one another, liked one another, worn the same sort of clothes, and so on. Young Herbert didn't work it out quite in that way, but anything was better than venturing into those wide, cultivated acres where private enterprise held sway.

So, to the canal he went, with an old bucket and one of Mrs. Pinnegar's less rusty table knives. Right at the start he had to learn the lesson that comes to every gardener: all the flowers are never out at the same time. Either you are too late or you are too early. The flowers you grow today are never so lovely as the flowers you grew yesterday and will grow again tomorrow. The gardener is a frustrated being for whom flowers never bloom at the right moment. Change and decay in all around he sees. It is all very sad, and how gardeners manage to keep going in the face of such adversities is one of those things that no fellow will ever understand.

Young Herbert had made a list of the flowers he would include in his prize posy. There were yellow flags, meadow-sweet, mimulus, cuckoo flowers, ragged robins, lords and ladies, and, of course, wild forget-me-nots. When it came to the point, he had to cross so many names off his list that there seemed to be nothing left. This was terrible. Young Herbert sat down on the bank with his bucket and, as many a gardener has done, mourned that he couldn't pack all summer into one August afternoon.

Still, there were the forget-me-nots and the creeping jenny, and the meadow-sweet. He was doubtful about the mimulus; it looked as though it would fade almost before he got it home. That was the trouble with water-flowers. They didn't last anything like so well as those you picked in the fields. It was like trying to keep minnows alive; you had to be always changing the water three or four times before you got them home. Well, it couldn't be helped. Young Herbert filled his bucket with a bit of everything and hoped for the best.

On the morning of the show, he woke up at six o'clock to find it raining; pouring heaven's hard; a real soaker. Last night, when they walked round the tents and peeped into the caravans, you would have thought it would keep fine for a week. Everybody said so, even old Noah Boulton who could smell rain a mile off. And here it was, coming down in great drops. . . .

If young Herbert had been a bit older, he would have known that this was the best thing that could have happened. "Rain before seven, fine before eleven"; plenty of time for it to dry up before the judges went round and the big cricket match started. But Youth doesn't trust Experience. This was the Day and there was the Rain. So a small boy, as so many small boys had done before him, turned his face to the wall, and wept.

This was not the only shock on that eventful day. When he got to the big tent he found to his dismay that his bunch of wild flowers, carefully arranged in a large pie-dish, was about half the size of any other exhibit. Foxgloves, golden mulleins and sweet rocket towered above his poor little effort. Where he had collected less than a dozen varieties, his competitors had twenty. Young Herbert felt an awful sinking in his stomach. So this was where his fear of the farmers had landed him. Well, it served him right. But you lived and you learned; he'd know better next time.

Exhibitors were putting the last touches to vegetables, fruit and flowers—one was polishing a rosy apple with a bit of flannel—when the Judges came in and ordered all competitors out of the tent. These olympians, who came from neighboring villages, filled everyone with awe. Serious-looking men, they brought with them an air of solemnity suitable to such a solemn occasion. Young Herbert hung around as long as he dared, watching them pinch marrows, cut apples into halves, make entries in little books. . . . And, as he watched, he made his great resolve. One day, he, too, would be a judge at a flower show. One day, he would know so much about flowers that he would be asked to judge at all the shows. They would drive over for him in a tall dogcart, and invite him to sit at the top table in the big luncheon tent. Perhaps he would have to make a speech. . . .

He was so busy building his castles in the air that he

quite forgot the disaster of the wild flower competition. It was a minute or two, also, before he noticed that the Judges—that imposing collection of autocrats—were accompanied by the most lovely, laughing lady he had ever seen. Almost a girl she was; not a day older than eighteen—young Herbert stood in the center of the tent with his mouth wide open and promptly fell in love, for ever, and ever, amen.

Failing to take precautions, he was discovered and bundled out of the tent with a flea in his ear. Not that that mattered. Here was one of those great lovers, knocked sideways, endways and all of a heap. "Gold in her hair, gold at her feet. . . ." Young Herbert wandered out into the bright sunshine, fell over a guy-rope and nearly broke his neck. But it was worth it.

For the next two hours he rambled round the fair playing the delicious game of choosing what you would do if you had the money to do it. When no one was looking, he tried the strength-testing machine, but as he couldn't lift the mallet, he passed on to look at the pig which was being smothered in grease and would become the property of anyone who could catch it. Later he sat down under a tree and ate the sandwiches Mrs. Pinnegar had packed for him—winding up finally as a spectator at the cricket match which was always played on the afternoon of the show.

He was lying on the grass at the side of the pavilion when a wonderful young man in white flannels and a pink blazer called out to him: "Hi, youngster, run and fetch something for this lady to sit on." Staggering back with a deck chair as large as himself, young Herbert was rewarded with the first sixpence he had ever owned—and a smile from the laughing lady of the flower tent. After which, he dashed off into the fair, to lose himself among the roundabouts and the swings. Forgotten, the cricket match; forgotten, the wild flower competition. Young Herbert, with sixpence in his pocket and a strange bumping under his corduroy jacket was the happiest boy in the show.

Some hours later, when the sun was beginning to dip behind the great elms of the park, everybody gathered round the pavilion, where the prizes were to be handed to the lucky winners. Young Herbert had no particular interest in this, but when he saw who was distributing the half-crowns, the shillings and the sixpences, he squeezed through into the front row to have another good look at his lovely lady. One by one the villagers walked up the steps, received their prizes and were duly clapped by the less fortunate. There was old Mrs. Edmonds, who made the best dough cakes in the world, and the conductor of the local band, who had coached his boys to victory in the tug-of-war. Almost everybody seemed to have a prize except young Herbert. But what did *he* care.

And then: "Wild Flower Competition for school children under the age of twelve: First Prize, Herbert Pinnegar. . . ." The lovely lady stood with a little white envelope in her hand, but no one came forward to take it. Its rightful owner, the small boy in the front row, was far away in a golden country where knights rode on white horses and pushed spears into one another. Someone gave him a push in the back. "Get on wi' it; that be you!" said a voice and young Herbert was literally shoved up the steps. . . .

"Well, well!" said the lady, "it's the little boy who got me the chair. That was very nice of you. Do you know why I've given you the first prize?"

"No, miss," said young Herbert. And if ever he spoke the truth, it was then.

"Because you picked water flowers instead of grabbing the first things that came and mixing them up anyhow. You must help me with my garden one of these days. . . . Now, run along. . . ."

He should, of course, have touched his cap, turned smartly round, run down the steps and showed his bright new half-crown to his envious contemporaries. But young Herbert did none of these things.

He just stood there and whimpered wretchedly.

"Didn't even hold out his hand for the money," as one incredulous matron remarked to a neighbor.

But the winner of the second prize was waiting, so he was bustled down the steps and the whole unfortunate episode was attributed to an attack of nerves, common to the very young in our more remote rural districts.

But nerves had nothing to do with it. Conscience had reared its frightening head. Young Herbert wanted to explain to the lady how it wasn't cleverness but fear of the farmers that had won him the prize. In his heart he knew that he had deceived her, and he would never forgive himself for that. . . .

No, not if he lived to be a hundred, he wouldn't.

And, to do him justice, he never did.

CHAPTER FIVE

Summer, that year, ran through into winter without a break. No rain fell, lawns cracked and you could have swept the bed of the county brook with a broom. Never in living memory had there been such a summer.

Crops were light, but as there was no waste the yield was well above the average. Prices were down, but so was the cost of clearing the fields under such ideal conditions. All was safely gathered in; and everybody was happy.

The village boys had the time of their lives. As the rabbits began to bolt from the dwindling corn, they ran and shouted to their hearts' content. Once in a while, a young rabbit, scared by the noise, would hide under a sheaf and be caught by some urchin not much bigger than itself. Very occasionally, a lucky shot with a prong handle would account for another, but, for the most part, the wild creatures were more frightened than hurt.

The only person who did not share in the general holiday spirit was the farmer's wife. During the greater part of the year she had all the help she wanted in the garden and in the house. She could always count on one of the stable lads to do a bit of digging, and the women from the cottages would always come along to help with the weekly wash. But now they were all busy in the fields. The boys were leading the horses to and from the rickyard; the women were setting up the sheaves and even the children were doing a bit of leazing on their own account. The carnival of harvest caught up casual labor in its hungry clutches and no drones were tolerated in that busy human hive.

So that when the farmer, worried and harassed by the rush of events, came upon young Herbert thoughtfully dissecting a moon daisy, he had something to say about it. The farmer had just had a bit of a wigging from his wife, because there was no one to carry her water-cans, so he sent the idle young loafer to report at the back door, and to look slippy about it.

Young Herbert looked as slippy as his game leg allowed. To tell the truth, he was rather glad to help in the garden; not because there would be a penny or two at the end of it, but because it hurt him to see the flowers suffering for want of a drop of water at the end of a hot day. So he filled a couple of buckets at the pump in the courtyard, and staggered round to where the farmer's wife was busy with her watering-can.

She welcomed him with open arms. "Bless the boy," she said, "I was driven out of my wits and *you* come along. Now we can get the job done in half the time." Young Herbert glowed with pleasure. Here was a job worth doing and someone worth helping. He put his back into it, and the buckets came round the corner with the speed and precision of a modern conveyor belt.

The farmer's wife was impressed. An enthusiast herself,

she recognized enthusiasm in others. In between the journeyings to the pump, she talked of seed boxes, of cold frames, of bedding out and of how a border should be arranged. Here you put the lobelia and there the smaller phlox, which had to be pegged down to run along the ground. Behind came the asters, the stocks with their lovely scent and the velvety salpiglossis. If you had geraniums, so much the better, but the annuals made a good show on their own account.

The farmer's wife was conservative in her tastes and habits. There was a routine about these things, just as night followed day and the moon came up when the sun went down. Beyond a bit of laurel and the big golden-chain tree, she had never heard of flowering shrubs and similar vanities. Pink may was an innovation and white lilac was yet to come. But, in her narrow limits, she was unrivaled. A craftsman of the old school.

Are you old enough, or wise enough to remember and appreciate those country gardens of the early 'eighties? The moss rose under the kitchen window; the sweet williams, all of one homely pattern; the great cabbage roses and the musk that had not yet lost its scent. Mignonette flourished in the poor, gravelly soil under the holly tree; maidenhair fern carpeted the gray steps of the old summer house and lilies of the valley grew like weeds.

Are we deceiving ourselves when we believe that blight, and similar garden pests, are modern inventions of a modern devil, unknown in that original Eden? Certainly there were snails, because we chased them by candle-light, with an old horn lanthorn, and small boys were given a penny a hundred, for catching them in the hour before bedtime. But that was only because gardens were watered as they have never been watered since, in spite of those modern spraying and whirling gadgets displayed in such plausible profusion at the agricultural shows.

It meant hard work, back-aching work; carrying endless buckets; kneeling on an old sack half the time and eternally planting out those sturdy little annuals grown in the leaf mold from the shrubbery at the bottom of the garden. Every year, the leaves from the nut bushes were collected in a heap, and every spring the fine mold was passed through a sieve, to be ready for the seed boxes placed end to end in the frame under the old brick wall. After which, the whole back-aching business began all over again. You had to love it, or you wouldn't have got away with an aching back; it would have broken your heart into the bargain.

Into this strenuous world, young Herbert fell headlong—and he loved every minute of it. Having carried buckets of water until he could scarcely stand, he asked if he could come again tomorrow night. "Bless the boy," said the farmer's wife, "of course you can come tomorrow"; and when she blessed the boy for the second time in one evening, she really meant it. Offered the usual penny, the young gardener refused it. "But why not?" asked the puzzled lady. "Because," he replied, "I like coming." In his philosophy, work was doing what you didn't want to do, and work was the only thing you got paid for.

So the long summer evenings passed in a placid atmosphere of mutual content. Everybody was happy. Even Mr. Bellman, the farmer, coming in from the fields and finding his supper ready on time, was as happy as he knew how to be. Not that he noticed any difference in the garden. Husbands never notice anything their wives have been doing during the day—especially where flowers are concerned. You can work your fingers to the bone, fill all the vases and shift the sofa round to the other side of the fireplace; but does a man suddenly leap into the air, half stunned by the wonder of it all? Does he? He does not.

In this little war of the sexes, young Herbert was on the side of the ladies. He could not, for the life of him, imagine how the farmer could come into his garden and not appreciate all that had been done for it. The lobelia now made an endless chain all round the edge of the border; the stocks scented the night air and you never saw such asters in your life. Yet the farmer would walk right through the middle of it without turning his head. The man didn't deserve to have a garden. It would serve him right if all the flowers vanished, leaving nothing but a square patch of bare ground—except, of course, that he would plant it with turnips and like it better than ever.

But, as summer faded, young Herbert had something more serious to worry about. First, the days began to draw in and there was no time for watering, even if it was needed, which it wasn't. Then, one morning, all the dahlias went black, killed off by the first frost. Finally, the men came in from the harvest field and, during the slack period before Christmas, casual laborers were two a penny. If the farmer didn't know what to put a man at, he told him to report to the missus, who was supposed to want help in the garden. They came with great forks and spades and elbowed the young interloper out of the way, until he was driven to seek refuge in the tool shed.

How he hated them, tearing up his beloved garden as though it was no better than a plowed field. It wasn't so bad, so long as they stuck to the kitchen garden, but when they set about the flower borders, scattering bulbs and the roots of precious perennials all over the place, young Herbert could have killed them. Once again he vowed that he would never, never go on to a farm. They could beat him, starve him, send him to the workhouse, but a farm laborer he would never be. When they had gone, he went round picking up the poor victims and returned them safely to their parent soil.

But it was one thing to have big ideas and quite another to put them into practice. You couldn't talk yourself out of a trap. Christmas was coming, and young Herbert was due to leave school at the end of the term. What was going to happen then? Everybody supposed he would go on the land, like all the other boys. It didn't seem to occur to anybody that you might not want to work on a farm. If the boys didn't go on the farm, who would do the work? What else was there to do, anyway; and what else was he good for? As he lay in bed at night, all these queries took goblin shape and gibbered at him from the bed-rail.

At the end of the term, it was customary for boys who were leaving school to go along to the Vicarage and have a nice friendly little chat with the chairman of the governing body. You were shown into the study, where the Vicar sat behind his big desk and you answered one or two questions on the Travels of St. Paul or the Sermon on the Mount—just to make sure that you were fitted for the great business of life. Then the Vicar asked what you were going to do and you mumbled that you were going into the stables up at the farm. After which, the Vicar patted you on the shoulder, gave you a new sixpence and you went out into the world.

When young Herbert's turn came to take the plunge, something went wrong with the usual routine. In the first place, the Vicar was not alone. Sitting in an armchair, reading a copy of a magazine, was the lady of the flower show. By this time, everybody knew that she was going to marry young Captain Charteris, who had bought the Manor, and that the wedding was taking place almost any day now. Being thus occupied, the Vicar cut out his usual preamble and got down to business.

"Well, Pinnegar," he said, "what are you going to do?"

Young Herbert shifted from one foot to another. "I dunno, sir," he replied.

This breaking with tradition was rather disturbing. "But, surely," said the Vicar, "they'll find you work on the farm, in—ah—some capacity?"

"No, sir," said young Herbert.

"But you *want* to go on the land, don't you?" prompted the Vicar.

"No, sir," said young Herbert.

This simple negative had various repercussions. Young Herbert could scarcely believe his ears when he heard himself talking such treason. The Vicar literally gaped with astonishment. And the lady sat there, laughing at the pair of them, until the tears ran down her cheeks.

She was the first to speak. "But, Vicar," she said, "why should he have to go on the land if he doesn't want to?"

Recovering his composure, the Vicar gave the official ruling: "All the village boys go on the land. Otherwise, where should we get our carters and our cowmen of tomorrow? The land needs them. They have been educated with that end in view. I will speak to Bellman . . ."

The young lady, who had been considering this strange child, suddenly interrupted. "Aren't you the boy who won the prize for wild flowers at the show?"

"Yes, miss," replied young Herbert.

"Of course you are. The only one who showed any imagination. You're fond of flowers, aren't you?"

"Yes, miss," gulped young Herbert.

"How would you like to come to the Manor, and help me with my new garden?"

The gates of Paradise opened widely on well-oiled hinges and then, as slowly, closed again.

"Really, Charlotte," said the Vicar, "I wish you wouldn't interfere. What do you know of our rural problems? You've only been here two minutes."

"If it comes to that, Vicar," was the surprising reply, "what do *you* know about the Garden of Eden? You were never there at all."

CHAPTER SIX

Young Herbert—and this is the last time he will be so described—started on his first job early in the New Year.

This tremendous occasion, anticipated with a fearful joy passing the understanding of all but the fledgling concerned, raised scarcely a ripple on the placid waters of village life. Bert Pinnegar rose early, put vaseline on his hair, refused his morning bread and dripping, and reported for duty in the Manor garden half an hour before his new world was really awake.

Wearing his Sunday suit, he looked rather like a young starling that had fallen out of its nest. Especially so when he perched on the corner of a cold frame waiting for the worst that could happen to him. There he was discovered by Mr. Addis, the head gardener, who viewed him with a disfavor bordering upon actual dislike.

Mr. Addis had two boys cluttering up the place already; and Mr. Addis had a theory about boys. One boy was a boy; two boys was half a boy and three boys was no boy. Furthermore, Mr. Addis had not been consulted. What with the wedding and going on the honeymoon, his new mistress had quite forgotten to mention to her head gardener that she had made an addition to his staff. That was a nice start! Mr. Addis supposed he would very soon have half the worthless young varmints in the village dumped on to him.

Mr. Addis was a kind man and a good man. But he knew his place and he expected others to betray a similar awareness of a head gardener's unhappy lot. One of the old-fashioned sort, he took his job seriously. He liked to give satisfaction, and how could he give satisfaction if everybody was pulling against him, as you might say? All these things he explained, patiently and with some warmth, to Bert Pinnegar, who had now taken his hands out of his pockets and was standing smartly to attention.

Besides, concluded Mr. Addis, how could he spare the time to teach a beginner all there was to learn—even supposing that beginner was willing to learn; which he, Mr. Addis, very much doubted? Was he, Bert Pinnegar, willing to learn all that he, Mr. Addis, was willing to teach him?

Bert Pinnegar replied that he knew "quite a bit, a'ready."

"Ho, ho!" chuckled Mr. Addis. "Then perhaps you'll be able to teach *me* a thing or two?"

Mr. Addis did not intend this to be taken literally. It was not his considered opinion that Bert Pinnegar could teach him anything; but his new assistant had come from a place where people said what they meant and meant what they said. He considered this trifle of jocularity with some care, before venturing an opinion.

"I don't know," he said. "I'll try."

It took Mr. Addis a week to get over that. Indeed, they had not had what you might call a cozy little chat together by the time the honeymoon was over and the new mistress had returned to the Manor. But Mr. Addis was a fair man. He had seen Bert Pinnegar nipping around; had even caught him working overtime; so, when asked how the new boy was getting along, he replied that, given time, they might make something of him.

Mr. Addis was a fair man. He would tell you himself, more than once, that he did unto others as he would they should do unto him. Also, he had a weakness for small boys who worked overtime when there was a job to be finished. So he put his pride in his pocket and let bygones be bygones. This was, perhaps, as well, for the time came, though not yet, when Mr. Addis learned more from Bert Pinnegar than either of them realized.

In the 'eighties, English gardens had achieved a restful homeliness lying about midway between the elegance of the past and the professional competence of the future. Vistas, parterres and classical shrines had faded into the landscape. The modern marvels of the Chelsea Flower Show were yet to come. Life was placid, unimaginative and rather pleased with itself. There were no new worlds worth conquering. No urge, no rush, no worries. The sort of world that bred the sort of man Mr. Addis was proud to be.

It was the age of established things, when a man was not ashamed to say that what was good enough for father was good enough for him. Whiskers and wisdom were so mixed up you couldn't tell one from the other. Lord Salisbury had a beard; W. G. Grace had a beard and if Mr. Gladstone had had a beard, he would have been a better man. Mr. Addis had a beard; Mr. Addis may have had more whiskers than wisdom, but he had been head gardener at the Manor for thirty years and there would be no shifting him until they carried him away in his coffin. A *sound* world.

But not the sort of world in which a young man could win his spurs overnight. Promotion was slow, and the position, when you achieved it, was secure. You didn't change your job every two minutes, and the young fellow coming up behind you had to wait his turn, the same as you had had to do. That was all right for the old fellows, but not so good for the young chaps with their way to make in the world. Some of them tried to force the pace by growing beards when they were seventeen, but this deceived nobody. Bert Pinnegar tried to grow a beard, but Mr. Addis sent him home to wash his face, and he had to wait like the others.

That was the trouble. The old fellows hung on, doing the same thing in the same way, and not a new idea among the lot of them. Rule of thumb, they called it; and they got away with it because you never could tell what the whiskers were hiding. More beards than brains, most of them. Hung on to the best jobs, getting more and more contraptious every day; until, finally, they went down with rheumatics and their places were taken by better men. But even then they weren't satisfied. They would sit outside their cottages, scolding the world like an old crow at the top of an elm tree. Always orating about something, they were, but, as nobody listened, there was no great harm done.

Mr. Addis had not yet reached this last deplorable stage in life's journey. He was getting on, but he still had a lot of kick left in him. Leaning heavily on tradition, he allowed no unfortunate experiments to shake his authority, and his young men, however they might grumble in secret, were quick to learn that what was good enough for Mr. Addis was good enough for them.

There was a lot of good in Mr. Addis, make no mistake about that. The respect he claimed from others was based firmly on the respect he paid to his job. He loved a lawn. A plantain on one of his lawns gave him more pain than a boil under his collar stud. One day, when Bert Pinnegar was wheeling a barrow towards the dump, he saw Mr. Addis standing, like a statue of Lord Wellington, in the center of one of his lawns. Mr. Addis had seen something and called him over to have a look at it.

"What," asked Mr. Addis, "is *that?*"

"A daisy," said young Pinnegar, wheeling his barrow across the sacred sward. "Pretty, isn't it? First I've seen this year."

For three-quarters of a split second, Mr. Addis surveyed his trusted lieutenant with a speculative eye. Then he made the sort of noise he had made on the day that the bee got into his beard—and Bert Pinnegar fled with his barrow in the direction of the dump, where he remained until driven forth by the pangs of hunger, two hours later.

Among his many great qualities, Mr. Addis had a straight eye and a rare sense of color. His daffodils marched two abreast along a road that was the shortest distance between two fixed points. No stragglers. No little clumps bivouacking in some sunny corner. To plant them, you had a long string with its ends fastened to a couple of pegs, and when the string was stretched to its fullest extent, the bulbs were placed along it at regular intervals. Naturalized daffodils that grew under the hedges and round the apple trees in the orchard were of no account—like gypsies, drovers, and other nondescripts of the human race.

Tulips were a bit more trouble, for here the color question came into it. You not only had to get them into straight lines, but you had to see that the reds didn't get mixed up with the yellows, and so on. Once, when the labels on the bags of bulbs got all mixed up, the border under the south wall was a riot. All the colors ran into one another like a rainbow, and there was the hell to pay. Mr. Addis raged up and down, like a wounded buffalo at bay—until someone said how lovely the tulips looked and then he pretended he had done it on purpose. Artful old fox!

But, taking all in all, Bert Pinnegar got a good grounding in his new job. He learned that gardening is the hardest work in the world. The young fellows on the farm reckoned that he had a cushy job; all you had to do was stick a few plants in and let them grow. Now and then you pulled up a few weeds, mowed a lawn or two and did a bit of watering in the evenings. In the autumn you brushed up the leaves and all winter you sat in the greenhouses, where it was nice and warm. And you got paid for it. What a life!

Sometimes, when Bert Pinnegar had been scratching about on his hands and knees for a couple of hours, he almost felt it in his heart to envy his late school-fellows who led horses at plow, helped the shepherd with the hurdling and rode back to the farm on the tail of a dung cart. Pulling the cord of a mowing machine could be dull work and as for plantains—their roots were so persistent that you never seemed to come to the end of them. Bert

Pinnegar reckoned they must start growing in Australia and that one day, when the hole was deep enough, he would come face to face with a black man.

But such moments of depression were few. Gardening may be the most exasperating occupation under the sun, but it gives as much as it gets—no more no less. Life in a garden is one long war with the powers of Evil, but the victory is worth winning. Maddening catastrophes are followed by spectacular triumphs. One minute you are flat on your face, and the next you are soaring on the wings of the morning. Bert Pinnegar didn't express his feelings in those exact words, but something inside him kept singing the same sort of song.

It would be nice, of course, if the plaguy blight would leave the roses alone, or if the snails would stop biting the young clematis shoots, but you couldn't have everything. Curse of Eden, Mr. Addis called it; and he ought to know. . . .

He was the most plaguy old pest of the lot.

CHAPTER SEVEN

At the age of sixteen, Bert Pinnegar fell in love for the last time.

Up at the house there was an under-housemaid. A lovely little thing. Her face had the perfect oval of a filbert nut and the hair that tumbled across it was the color of ripe corn. Her eyes, and the way she used them, knocked men all of a heap—and made women want to smack her. She had a wicked little mouth and no chin to speak of. . . .

That was Soph.

Already the housekeeper had an eye on her. "Mark my words," she said, "that girl will come to no good. Knows too much by half for a child her age. Any nonsense from her, and back she goes to her mother."

"Nice enough little thing," hazarded young William, recently promoted to a green apron and care of the silver. Mrs. Garlick was down on him like a brick. "Now, young William, I don't want any more of that from you. Allow me to know my own sex, and keep your eyes off my girls. *I've* seen them hanging round the pantry, giggling like a lot of silly sparrows."

"They should have been doing the bedrooms," said William.

"They should," agreed Mrs. Garlick.

"And what," asked William, innocently, "what would you have said to me if I'd sent your girls about their business?"

"There's reason in all things," announced the housekeeper, with quiet dignity, "but since you ask me, William, the less you see of my girls the better I shall be pleased."

So that when next young Soph poked her nose round the pantry door, in search of a little attention, she got more than she bargained for. Something seemed to have upset William; as a rule she could twist him round her little finger. Ah, well, he'd come round—they all did.

Baffled—but unbowed—Soph hatched up an excuse that would take her into the gardens. There she found Bert Pinnegar, picking off the dead pansy blossoms and fearing no evil.

"Lovely, aren't they!" she murmured. "All their little faces looking up at you."

Bert Pinnegar hadn't much time for girls, but anyone who loved a garden walked straight into his heart. He asked her if she was fond of flowers and she replied that she thought they were ever so nice. It must be wonderful to know all about flowers, the same as Bert Pinnegar did. She'd always wanted to work in the garden, but she'd never had the chance. One day she was going to have a garden, all her own, where she could dig—and dig—and dig. . . . What flowers did Bert Pinnegar like best?

The young gardener sat back on his heels and considered this problem. It was the first time he had been approached as an expert and it was up to him to do his best. Here was a kindred spirit, a true lover of flowers, who had been robbed of the advantages he enjoyed. Besides, now he came to look at her . . .

Bert Pinnegar hadn't much time for girls, but when you had one dumped right on top of you, so to speak; and when she asked your advice about things, *and* had hair like ripe corn—well, that made a difference. He thought for a minute and then gave it as his considered opinion that there was a lot to be said for these new begonias, so long as you didn't let the frost get them in the winter.

"That's funny," said Soph, "I like begonias better'n anything. I love begonias, I think they're ever so nice."

Rather elementary flattery this, but nobody had bothered to flatter Bert Pinnegar before. It was new—and it was nice. Here was a little slip of a thing who had more sense in her head than any girl he had met. Pity someone couldn't take her in hand and make something of her. He didn't hold with women gardeners—or, rather, Mr. Addis didn't—but this girl, given a chance . . .

Soph was kneeling down beside him on the bit of sacking; very close to him she was, and a wisp of corn-colored hair tickled his ear. He hadn't much time for girls, but this was different. As he had been given *his* chance, so she should have hers. Perhaps, if he gave her a few tips, she would learn enough to make a start. Why not begin now?

"You'll have to look out for the mice," he said. And, with that, the spell was broken. The earnest seeker after truth leapt into the air, as though she had been sitting on an emmets' nest.

"What's the matter?" asked Bert Pinnegar.

"Mice!" cried Soph. "You said there was mice. They scares me out of my life they do." And she was gone before he could explain that begonia corms were stored in the attics; which swarmed with mice; which were particularly partial to begonia corms. If she was going to be a proper gardener, it was good that she should know these things.

Soph was always in and out of the garden after that. What with William still having the grumps, and Mrs. Garlick giving them the rough end of her tongue, a quiet chat behind the tool shed came as a welcome relief. Bert Pinnegar had made it all right about the mice. The open-air sort, he explained, were quite harmless; not really mice at all, they weren't, but she'd have to get used to them, if she reckoned to be a proper gardener. Then he passed firmly on to Lesson Six—*The Use of Manures and Fertilizers in a Garden*—to which his pupil listened with the rapt attention of an almost-engaged girl at a Rugger match, who wishes she had brought another coat and wonders what the hell it is all about, anyway.

Not that Bert Pinnegar was entirely immune to feminine charm. It was warm and comforting to have a girl cuddle up to you; made you feel you really were somebody. So, when the temptress began to come into the open, she found an easy victim.

Soph had a genuine passion for flowers—of the right sort. Not the ordinary kind you found all over the place, like mignonette, sweet williams and silly snapdragons, but the more showy sorts that only grew under glass. She would stand with her nose pressed against the pane of a greenhouse, imagining herself sweeping into a ballroom, smothered in orchids.

One day, Mr. Addis caught her playing this game and was about to fetch her a crack across her behind with a spud, when she saw his reflection in the glass. "Oh, Mr. Addis," she said, "what wonderful flowers you do grow. Can anybody else grow such wonderful flowers as you do, Mr. Addis? I think they're ever so nice."

"Humph!" grunted Mr. Addis, sticking his spud into an imaginary dandelion; and Soph made good her escape. What silly things men were. You could always get round them, if you stroked them the right way. All except William. She couldn't think what had happened to William lately; always snapping at you. Oh, well, there were just as good fish in the sea as ever came out of it.

Meanwhile, there was always Bert Pinnegar, silly young idiot, droning on about lawns and lupins. Gave her the jumps, having to listen to all that rubbish. Never mind, she wouldn't have to put up with it much longer. The dance was tomorrow, and if she hadn't got her orchids out of him by then . . .

The next morning, Bert Pinnegar learned that as there are maggots in the core of a Blenheim Orange, so there is evil in the heart of a maid. With Mr. Addis safely out of the way, Soph got him into a corner and demanded the price of her devotion. She was going to a dance and she had got to have orchids. Other girls had orchids; you saw them in the magazines, you read about them in books. She would meet him outside the back door at six o'clock and if he hadn't got them with him, then that was the finish of everything. The victim wriggled a bit, but he had met his match. Soph went to the dance and she took her orchids with her.

Who told who, and which of the village gossips told

the housekeeper at the Manor did not transpire, but Mrs. Garlick knew all about it next morning. She sent for her under-housemaid and asked who gave her the orchids.

"Bert Pinnegar," replied Soph, who told the truth when it suited her. The housekeeper sent her compliments to the head gardener, and could he spare young Pinnegar to do a bit of a job in the house?

Mr. Addis could, and did. The Inquiry was short. Bert Pinnegar admitted taking a spray of orchids. Had Mr. Addis given him permission? He had not. Was the spray already broken off by any chance? It was not. Why had he done such a dreadful thing? No answer. The housekeeper was considering her next question, when the door opened to admit the Lady of the House—the lady of the flower show—the timely visitor at the Vicarage. But, today, Bert Pinnegar wished her at the other end of the world, and farther away than that.

"Dear me," she said. "Is anything the matter?"

The housekeeper gave her the findings of the Inquiry. Young Pinnegar had been caught stealing orchids from the greenhouse. He had given them to one of the under-housemaids, who had worn them at a dance, to the scandal of the entire neighborhood.

"Did you ask him to do it?" asked the Lady, turning to young Soph.

"No, ma'am, certainly not. I wouldn't think of doing such a thing."

"Then why did he give them to you?" asked the Lady.

"Trying to get round me, he was. Always pestered me, he has; ever since he's been here," said young Soph, shaking her corn-colored hair out of her candid blue eyes. It was an old trick and had got her out of more scrapes than this; but, somehow, it didn't seem to be going down so well this time. Indeed, the Lady wasn't looking. Just thinking, she was. When she spoke, it was to the housekeeper.

"You know, Mrs. Garlick," she said, "I've often thought we start these young girls earlier than we should. They aren't quite old enough to be out in the world. They should be at home with their mothers and come to us later. Tell her to pack her bag and we'll send her home in the morning."

"But I don't want to go home," screamed young Soph. "I'm not a kid any more and my mother's an old faggot; I hate her . . . I hate all of you . . . I hate everybody . . ."

"And what," asked the housekeeper, "are madame's views concerning young Pinnegar?"

"Madame has no views concerning young Pinnegar," was the reply, "except that little boys sometimes do very silly things—and are very sorry for them afterwards. I expect Mr. Addis will talk to him."

CHAPTER EIGHT

Mr. Addis talked to young Pinnegar with the end of a strap, until his arm ached; and young Pinnegar took it in very good part. Indeed, he welcomed it, for it left him with a nice clean feeling, as one who had received absolution after paying penance for his crime.

Back in the 'eighties the inhabitants of these islands were still a primitive race, indulging in excesses of cruelty and superstition. In our more enlightened age we realize that corporal punishment brutalizes the young offender, and that coercion in any form is to be deprecated. Mr. Addis did not know this. He gave young Pinnegar a damned good hiding; and, as gardening is not a sitting-down job, no great harm was done.

But the incident had its repercussions, nevertheless. Love, like the measles, may be unpleasant while it lasts, but it inoculates its victim against further attack. You very rarely get it twice. Now and again you may feel a twinge of the old enemy, but you hardly ever come out in spots a second time. Bert Pinnegar, at the age of sixteen, had said good-bye to all that. Which left him with time on his hands.

The love life of a village boy is less complicated than that of an ant or an apricot. When the small boys tire of stealing sour apples and throwing stones at frogs, they get together in little groups and watch the stream of pedestrian traffic flow by. If it happens to be you, going to post a letter or taking the dogs for a run, they regard you solemnly from the moment you come into sight until you disappear round the corner. They never seem to be looking at anything (except you), or talking about anybody (except you), and if you speak to them they consider you with the owlish serenity of a stuffed fish.

You don't see village girls hanging about in groups like that. Either they stop at home and help their mothers with the younger children or they hunt in couples, waiting to winkle a couple of boys off the main group. All of which takes time and keeps the younger generation fully occupied.

Bert Pinnegar, having turned his back on romance, found himself at a bit of a loss. And so he fell into the habit of staying on in the garden after the others had gone; not from any sense of duty, but simply because he didn't know what else to do with himself.

There was always something he could turn his hand to: a bit of watering, a bit of weeding, a rambler that had broken away from a wall. . . . The most difficult thing was to keep out of the way. He didn't want people to think he was hanging round where he wasn't wanted; so he flitted about like a little ghost, and many a time Mr. Addis, having made a note overnight of something that must be done, found in the morning that the fairies had been there before him.

Bert Pinnegar had not seen his Lady since that unfortunate affair in the housekeeper's room; but late one evening, when he was tidying up the edges of a grass path, she came round the corner. He didn't see her at first. He was so busy getting the curve just right that he wouldn't have noticed anything short of an earthquake.

"What are you doing there?" she asked.

"Nothingm'm," replied young Pinnegar, with the quick instinct of the small boy caught doing anything whatsoever.

"It looks very nice," said the Lady; "but isn't it rather late to be working? Did Mr. Addis tell you not to stop until you had finished the border?"

"Nom'm."

"But I can't have you working all hours of the day and night. What would people say? They'd call me a slave driver. You should be playing . . ."

So they were after him again. What business was it of theirs? Why wouldn't they leave him alone? He wasn't hurting anybody. Why should you have to stop doing something you liked, because it was called work; and start doing something you didn't like, because it was called play? "I like work better'n I like play," he muttered.

The Lady laughed. "What a funny little boy!" she said.

This upset Bert Pinnegar no end. Here was he, turning seventeen come next March, liable to start smoking any minute now; having to sit there and be called a funny little boy. Being laughed at. There were times when you had to speak up for yourself, and this was one of them.

"There's nothing to laugh at," he said. "I've seen *you* working in the garden and you don't get paid for it."

"That's different," she laughed. "No one would pay me. I'm only a beginner. I plant things upside down. You're a real gardener, so you shouldn't be expected to work for nothing."

"Nobody expects me to work for nothing—"

"Perhaps not, but when you stop on after hours in my garden I get something for nothing."

"You're kindly welcome," said young Pinnegar; and this time they both laughed.

The new Mrs. Charteris was one of those rare people who can accept favors with a good grace. She did not resent them as liberties or look for the catch in them. When young Pinnegar offered to work overtime for nothing she agreed, with the mental reservation that he wouldn't be the loser in the long run.

And so, the very next evening, you might have seen an oddly assorted couple toiling together in the Manor vineyard. The season was dry, and once again, as in the farmer's garden, most of the job consisted of carrying water-cans. But the labor was mixed up with delicious little talks about flowers and shrubs, in which young Pinnegar was most surprisingly able to hold his own. Indeed, Mrs. Charteris found some of her more nebulous theories blown sky-high.

Not that she had any great opinion of herself as a gardener. Coming from London, where flowers had bloomed for her in expensive West End shops, she had a lot to learn on the practical side. But she meant to be mistress in her own garden, and had built up from books a nice technical background, glittering with plausible theories, and riddled with those broad generalizations that come true once every so often.

Bert Pinnegar, on the other hand, dealt in facts, learned the hard way. He didn't plant things upside down because he had done that once, and wasn't likely to do it again. A course of Bert Pinnegar was good for Mrs. Charteris; and a course of Mrs. Charteris was more than good for Bert Pinnegar. . . .

Looking back on those quiet evenings in the Manor garden, Old Herbaceous reckoned that he owed everything to them. How else could he have got his tongue round all those Latin names? How could anyone hope to tackle a job like that if they hadn't been to college, and who ever heard of a working gardener going to one of those places? Yet his Lady could run off the most frightful tongue-twisters without turning a hair.

They played a sort of game together. Every evening she taught him a new word, and, if he didn't remember it the next night there was trouble—unless, of course, he could ask her one she didn't know, which made things all square.

He caught her out once after he had called a *fritillaria meleagris* a wild tulip.

"I'm surprised at you, Pinnegar," she said, "after all the trouble I've taken. You've got a head like an empty bucket."

That one went home; something had to be done about that. Empty bucket, indeed! And then, suddenly, just at the right minute, he remembered what Mary Brain had told him about those tall yellow flowers that look like foxgloves but aren't.

"When is a mullein not a mullein?" he asked.

Mrs. Charteris couldn't answer that one. She tried to wriggle out of it by saying that a mullein *was* a mullein. Then she gave up.

"When it's a verbascum," announced young Pinnegar. "Now who's got a head like an empty bucket?"

That was how it had all happened. Quite easily, in a spirit of fun, the small pilgrim had been led to the very gates of his Celestial City. For how can anyone become a proper gardener unless he can call flowers by their Latin names? Sitting among his cushions, Old Herbaceous was right in reckoning that he owed everything to those quiet evenings in the old Manor garden.

But that was only half the story. When he left the village school he was the scrubbiest little scrap of nothing that you ever saw. To match the dignity of his new position, they rigged him up in a pair of corduroy trousers, cut off at the knees and reaching up to his armpits. Not the sort of corduroy affected by Chelsea artists of a later day, but real honest stuff that lasted forever.

That was the trouble with corduroy—it lasted forever. Once you were in it, there was no getting out of it. A badge of servitude that kept you where you rightly belonged; tied to the tail of a dung cart. Of course you didn't have to be a plow boy all your life. You could become a carter, a cowman or a shepherd, but you never got out of the farm laborer class. Once corduroy had you in its grip, it never let go.

Young Pinnegar's main object in life was to get out of corduroy. He liked the warmth of it, but the feel and the smell of it made him sick. None of the Judges at the flower show had worn corduroy, and this had put them in a different world to the carters and cowmen who came long in the evening. Almost gentlemen they looked. Obviously, if you were going to be a proper gardener you had to get out of corduroy. But how?

Here again his Lady came to his relief. Mrs. Charteris, it seemed, had a young relation who grew out of his clothes before he had time to wear them. Actually, Mrs. Charteris had no such young relation, but she found the sort of outfitter who catered for the sort of person young Pinnegar, with proper handling, might become. Every now and again parcels of clothes, of a fairly homely pattern, would arrive, and young Pinnegar began to blossom as the rose.

And even that wasn't all. Viewed from a slightly snobbish angle, the village boy's vocabulary was limited and often deplorable. Mrs. Charteris was far too wise to attempt fancy tricks of the Pygmalion pattern. Beyond the occasional raising of an eyebrow at one of young Bert's more unfortunate *gaffes*, she allowed environment to work its inevitable cure.

So that, when the time came, Herbert Pinnegar was able to hold his own with anybody, as you might say.

CHAPTER NINE

Getting on in the world is never quite the happy business that young people suppose it will be.

Looking back, Old Herbaceous could remember very little of his next ten years, except that they weren't worth remembering. The first thrill of being allowed to work in a garden was over, and the joy of achievement was yet to come.

When a young fellow reached his twenties he was in a sort of doldrums, with flapping sails; becalmed, and likely to be so for the rest of his days. You never seemed to get anywhere and you never looked like getting anywhere. Like being at the bottom of a long ladder; every rung above you occupied and nobody moving. When you tried to work your way up the chap in front stepped on your fingers and told you to stop shoving.

And the jealousies. Some of the younger chaps, still in corduroys and likely to remain so, didn't take at all kindly to young Pinnegar's superior ways, and they weren't slow to let him know it. When there was a particularly dirty job to be done, like cleaning out the stokehole, they put him on to it, and laughed to see him making a mess of his fine new clothes. Rather like Joseph and his coat of many colors. Fortunately, the next parcel from London contained a set of blue overalls which, oddly enough, fitted him like a glove—and made his young tormentors more envious than ever.

Mr. Addis, too, was beginning to look at his youngest assistant down the side of his nose. Mr. Addis, having risen from the ranks, had also been baffled by the eternal problem of getting his tongue round all those Latin names. So that when young Pinnegar, in an expansive moment, referred to the Black-eyed Susans as *rudbeckia hirta*, he (Mr. Addis) got a severe jolt. Obviously he couldn't tick off the young upstart for impudence, as he would like to have done, but the incident left a scar.

Later on—much later on—Mr. Addis was glad to lean upon his young colleague in this matter of Latin names. Blaming a faulty memory, or pressure of more important affairs, he would hand over the labels and drift away in search of less intellectual pursuits. But not yet. Mr. Addis was still firmly seated in the saddle and needed no adventitious aids to keep him there.

Mrs. Charteris was also suffering from gardener's growing pains. There is something about a garden that brings out a fiercely possessive streak in the best of us. All our triumphs, to be really satisfying, must stem from our own individual efforts; and we look with a cold eye upon innovations for which we are not personally responsible. Even a suggestion, however tactfully introduced, is not always taken in good part. "Alone I did it," is the motto of all really keen gardeners; a sentiment which found its modern equivalent in the Army's laconic warning, "KEEP OUT! THIS MEANS YOU!"

We gardeners should not be blamed for this defensive attitude, which is based on the intense interest we take in our work. Without it, gardening would become an undertaking so laborious, so frustrating, so maddening, that there would soon be no gardens at all. As with all truly creative pursuits, the appeal is to the mind and to the heart, rather than to the pocket; and unless we can convince ourselves, beyond any doubt, that the credit is ours, and ours alone, we are like a singer listening to the applause for a song that someone else has sung.

Very well, then, Mrs. Charteris, having decided to be mistress in her own garden, was waking up to the fact that things weren't working out that way. First of all, Mr. Addis kept questioning her decisions, and now young Pinnegar was suggesting better ways of doing things. She stood it as long as she could, and then, on a small matter of carnation cuttings, she went up in smoke: "Very well," she said, "as you all seem to know better than I do, you'd better get on with it."

She didn't show her nose in the garden again for weeks. Actually, she had gone up to London to be presented to Queen Victoria, but Bert Pinnegar wasn't to know that. Robbed of his guardian angel, and blaming himself for being the cause of her departure, he wandered about like a lost soul. When she came back things were never quite the same; an easy comradeship being succeeded by the more normal relations existing between a considerate employer and an excellent member of an excellent staff.

So that, altogether, those early 'nineties were not so gay as people try to make out, though life in the Manor garden flowed on like a quiet stream. Year followed year and season followed season with quiet precision. No sooner was Christmas over than the first aconites began to push their heads through the fine leaf mold of the shrubbery floor. Faced by this annual phenomenon, Bert Pinnegar never stopped marveling at the early arrival of an English spring. He had always supposed that nothing happened in a garden until about March, yet here were these jolly little fellows in their frilled ruffs putting up as brave a show as a field of buttercups.

The naturalized daffodils in the orchard came up a lot earlier than those in the garden, and here again was an odd thing. Why were flowers under cultivation so much more delicate than the wild sorts? You would have thought, with all that time and care spent on them, that they would have stood up to anything. They were bigger, of course, but where was the sense of growing bigger flowers if they were always being destroyed by some bug or other? He could only suppose that the work you put into a garden to bring on the plants also brought out the pests. If that was so, was all the trouble worth while?

The apple blossom gave him his first real thrill. There was an old apple tree in the corner—a real old warrior that had seen its best days. Its fruit was almost worthless, but when it came into bloom it fairly made your heart stand still. Like the foam breaking on a reef of coral, it was. If Bert Pinnegar had been a poet, which he wasn't, he might have done better than that; but it was good enough to be going on with.

The pageant of summer! Almost too much of a good thing! Blossom flowed along the borders in great waves, and was gone. If only the thing would stop for half a minute and let you look at it. But no, it came and went; came and went; came and went; until there was nothing left but the Michaelmas daisies.

But perhaps he wasn't being quite fair. Bert Pinnegar always felt a little unhappy when finding fault with the ways of nature. Perhaps he didn't like summer because he hadn't time to enjoy all the good things. What with the mowing and cutting the edges, the days went by in a flash. Yes, that might be it. Anyhow, whatever the reason, summer was a bit disappointing, and always had been, as long as he could remember.

Autumn! Ah, now, that was better. For one thing, you mowed the lawns for the last time and put the mowing machine away until the spring. Lawns were all very well when you got someone else to do the work. He could understand Mr. Addis going potty about his lawns, but Mr. Addis didn't have to pull the roller. He (Bert Pinnegar) liked a nice lawn as well as anybody, but there were limits.

What he *really* liked about autumn was the smell of the chrysanthemums. That might seem a funny thing to say, but the smell of a chrysanthemum had a tang to it that fitted in with the season—like the smell of decaying leaves, and bonfires, and so on. Odd, no one else seemed to feel as he did about that. They talked about the scent of roses, and honeysuckle and tobacco plants, but many of them didn't know that a chrysanthemum had any smell to speak of. And chrysanthemums came at a time when they were really needed. What would you do about flowers for the house in October if it wasn't for them?

Flowers for the house! Bert Pinnegar was never one of those professional gardeners who go off the deep end if someone picks a few flowers to brighten up the drawing-room. He liked to see his mistress come out with a basket and a pair of secateurs—flitting here and there like a bee or a butterfly. No good being a dog in the manger about such things. And besides, some flowers looked a lot better when they were nicely arranged in a vase—gave you a chance to look at them properly. Especially the newer varieties, which didn't stand up to the weather and could be ruined in a night.

This applied particularly to spring flowers, which were knocked about by the March winds and splashed with mud during the April rains. Bert Pinnegar had a theory that while the semi-wild daffodils could be left to look after themselves, the garden sorts should be picked as soon as the buds showed a bit of color and brought into the house. Then you really had the best of them.

Which proves that, right up to the end of his days, Old Herbaceous had a bit of the child in him. Half the joy of flowers, for children, lies in picking them. You can't ask a small boy to leave all the violets on a sunny bank, or all the bluebells in a wood. Then why not pick flowers in a garden? Nothing to be said against it that he could see.

And so into winter. Bert Pinnegar never pretended that he had any use for a garden when it was frost-bound, any more than he liked it when it was burned up like a brick in the drought. Some people said a hard frost killed off the pests, but he wasn't so sure. That winter they had skating for six weeks was followed by the worst summer for pests that he could remember: blight on everything, a plague of wasps and hardly an apple without a maggot in it.

Give him a soft winter and he'd let the summer look after itself.

CHAPTER TEN

With the turn of the century things began to happen at last. Queen Victoria died, and the Prince of Wales became King of England—when it was almost too late to mean anything to him.

That's how it was in those days. The old folk hung on to their fat jobs until their sons were almost past work. Bert Pinnegar wasn't much of a reader, but, if he had been, he would have agreed with the new poem by Rudyard Kipling about people like Mr. Addis who thought they were alive when all the time they were really dead. . . . Here was he, at thirty, still being treated like a kid of no account. . . .

Just when he was most despondent Kruger began making trouble in South Africa, and one of the young fellows in the greenhouse was sent out to do something about it. Bert Pinnegar, being turned down for military service, got his job.

He wasn't too pleased at first. Since that affair with young Soph, he had kept away from the greenhouses. Also, he had the average countryman's mistrust of exotic things. These explorers, like Dr. Livingstone, went round the world and brought back strange, new plants, but what were they when you'd got them? Just a nuisance. Let the thermometer drop a couple of degrees and they were gone. Why, if one blossom happened to touch another, it was enough to ruin the both of them.

Still, you couldn't get anywhere without a knowledge of glass. A head gardener had to know a bit about everything, and if you didn't take on a job, somebody else did and got ahead of you. Bert Pinnegar took what the gods sent him, and tried to be thankful.

After all, glass was useful for bringing the stuff along, protecting some of the more delicate garden plants against bad weather, and so on. Mrs. Charteris was a rare one for having things a bit ahead of time; always chivvying them about that, she was. Most of the trouble with Mr. Addis was caused by him hanging on to the new beans until they were as long as your arm. Mr. Addis thought it was a waste of good stuff to send peas into the kitchen until they were really worth looking at—like the ones you saw at the shows.

And potatoes! Some people planted their seed potatoes long before Good Friday, because they liked them to come along early. That was all right if you didn't get a May frost, but if you did all your trouble was wasted. You wouldn't get Mr. Addis caught out that way. Mrs. Charteris tried everything under the sun to get her new potatoes, but Mr. Addis was always one too many for her. Either the ground was wrong for planting, or the seed potatoes were late coming down from Scotland. Then, if there *did* happen to be a frost, he would come along with a handful of blackened haulms and leave them on the kitchen table. Always out to rub it in, Mr. Addis was.

Bert Pinnegar was neutral in these wars. Not because he was afraid to take sides, but because he realized that it was just a gamble; like spinning a penny or backing a number at a fair. Some people liked to take a chance, and if they lost they had only themselves to blame. Mr. Addis, a good chapel man, didn't hold with gambling, and he had a right to his opinions; especially when he could quote Scripture ("their fruits in due season") to prove that he had the Lord on his side.

Thinking things over, Bert Pinnegar reckoned that there might, after all, be something to be said for glass. You couldn't start growing potatoes in a greenhouse, but what about strawberries? It nearly broke his heart to go out some morning, after a ground frost, and see those little black eyes in the middle of the blossom. A whole strawberry bed ruined in a night! Without saying anything to anybody, he planted half a dozen runners in pots and brought them into the greenhouse in October. But nothing happened. The plants just dwindled away, and nothing he could do would save them.

Then he remembered that strawberries had nothing to fear from the winter frosts. It was only when the blossom came that they ran into trouble. So the next year he waited until February and tried the experiment again.

In the meantime, Mrs. Charteris had been keeping an eye on his work in the greenhouses, and what she saw did not please her very much. Until now her policy of bringing him along by easy stages had shown excellent results, but he seemed, suddenly, to have come to a full stop. Either he was losing interest or, what was more likely, he lacked the education necessary for employment in a higher grade. Throughout that winter she watched him closely, offered suggestions and gave him every possible encouragement, but he never seemed to settle down in his new surroundings. Mrs. Charteris was puzzled, disappointed, and finally decided that she would have to make a change. Young Pinnegar had failed to make the grade.

Then a surprising thing happened. One afternoon, about the end of April, there was a pleasant little tea-party at the Manor. Nothing formal, of course, but not quite the casual affair that might happen on any day in the week. Just a gathering together of old friends to meet the estate solicitor who was down from London. Mrs. Garlick had been asked to put her best foot forward and, though she was getting on a bit now, had not done so badly. Having removed their cloaks and warmed themselves before the big open fireplace, the visitors were settling down to enjoy the good things when old General Henderson, his eyes popping out of his head, gave tongue like an old hound in cover.

"My god, Charlotte!" he cried, "where in heaven's name did you find *those*?"

Everyone turned to the General, except the hostess, who, warned by past experience, cast a furtive eye towards her tea-table. Everything seemed in order. The best tea-service, the silver kettle, Mrs. Garlick's admirable buttered scones. . . . What was the matter with the man?

"Strawberries!" roared the General. "Strawberries in April! What will you be giving us next?"

Mrs. Charteris thought the old warrior had gone mad —and then she saw them: a dish of such heavenly strawberries as neither Mr. Fortnum nor Mr. Mason had dreamed of in their most expensive moments. It was as though the year had taken a giant's stride forward, landing you suddenly in the last week of June. If the General was seeing things, so was his hostess. But she kept her head.

"Strawberries, General," she replied coolly, "just a few strawberries. Won't you try one?"

"But where did you get them?" asked three ladies in chorus.

Mrs. Charteris was asking herself the same question. But once again she kept her head. She rang her little silver bell, and the housekeeper, surprisingly on the alert, appeared in the doorway, to be asked, in tones that tried to appear casual, where the strawberries had come from.

"Pinnegar brought them in from the greenhouse five minutes ago," said Mrs. Garlick.

"Tell Pinnegar I wish to speak to him," said Mrs. Charteris; and, when Bert Pinnegar duly appeared in that holy of holies, wishing that the fine Bokhara carpet on which he was standing would waft him away to other climes, his mistress turned to the General:

"This is my gardener, General, he is in charge of the greenhouses and he knows all about such things. . . . Pinnegar, General Henderson would like to know how you manage to have strawberries ready for the table so early in the season."

So Bert Pinnegar explained, carefully and in simple terms, as you would to an intelligent child, how it had all happened. How it was no use starting the runners under glass in the autumn, because they got all dried up like, however much you watered them. What you had to do was to pot the runners in the autumn, leave them out in the open like the rest of the strawberries, and bring them into the greenhouse about February, so as to have them well under cover before they began to think about flowering. That was all there was to it.

General Henderson thanked Mr. Pinnegar for his very lucid explanation and Mr. Pinnegar was about to shuffle out backwards when his mistress landed her broadside before he could get out of range.

"Just a minute, Pinnegar," she said. "Which greenhouse did you use for this—interesting experiment?"

"The little one at the end, ma'am; next to the dump, ma'am."

"Strange. I've never seen strawberries growing there," said Mrs. Charteris.

"I put them under the bench whenever you were about," explained Mr. Pinnegar.

"Why did you do that?" asked Mrs. Charteris.

"Because," said Mr. Pinnegar, "I wanted it to be a surprise, like."

"Very well, Pinnegar, you may go."

Mr. Pinnegar went.

There is no suggestion here that Bert Pinnegar had made horticultural history. There was nothing new about forcing strawberries under glass fifty years ago, but his bit of original thinking paid dividends. Mrs. Charteris no longer thought about making a change. After all, the conventional greenhouse was getting into a rut, becoming a bit of a bore. Under the grandfatherly supervision of Mr. Addis you were inclined to get gloxinias—gloxinias

—and more gloxinias. Very nice, of course, but one gloxinia was very like another, and there wasn't much you could do about them. They just stood in rows and some were a bit bigger than others. Besides, now she came to think of it, she never had been all that keen on gloxinias. . . . And it had been rather sweet of Pinnegar—the way he produced strawberries out of his hat—like a conjuror. . . .

But it was the blue *Ipomées* that really won her over, as you might say. Mrs. Charteris, following in the footsteps of Queen Victoria, spent a holiday on the French Riviera. Staying in one of those great hotels at Cimiez, she visited the flower gardens of Grasse, and, during a little trip to Mentone spent an hour in the lovely grounds of La Mortola, just across the Italian frontier. Sir Thomas Hanbury, returning from the Far East with all the money in the world, had planted the promontory of Mortola with a wonderful collection of trees and shrubs —eucalyptus, agaves, casuarinas—and the gardens were esteemed as the loveliest in all Italy. Indeed, Queen Victoria had paid two visits, and on the second occasion had done a little sketching.

This being her first visit to a country enjoying a subtropical climate, Mrs. Charteris was thrilled by everything she saw. At one part of the coast were cork trees, waving bamboos, and umbrella trees. Little Moorish towns perched on the tops of hills, and, behind everything, the tideless Mediterranean shone like a great mirror. In one garden, attached to a quite ordinary villa, she saw bougainvillea, plumbago and the lovely "Belle de Nuit" growing in the open air. Geraniums grew like trees, and appeared to blossom all the year round. In fact, she felt that she was visiting the country described by Lord Tennyson, "Where falls not rain, nor hail, nor any snow—"

But it was the blue *Ipomée* that really made her heart stand still. When she was a little girl she had loved to grow "morning glories," and she had been encouraged to do so because it got her out of bed in good time. If you didn't look at them before breakfast you probably didn't see them at all, and the best of them faded by the middle of the morning. Grown-ups and gardeners were inclined to sniff at them, ranking them with the wild white convolvulus that clambered over the hedges in country lanes, but Mrs. Charteris, though she hadn't seen one for years, was still true to her childhood's favorite.

So that when she saw this Dawn Flower of the French Riviera for the first time, she could hardly contain herself. It rioted over everything, as though someone had torn great masses out of a morning sky. It was so blue, so blue that it positively hurt. She felt that her heart was being drowned in loveliness, and she could scarcely breathe.

A friend, noticing her odd behavior, asked anxiously if the heat was too much for her.

Mrs. Charteris was not feeling the heat. She felt that she was drifting over a blue sea, under a blue sky, into a lovely land of blue nothingness—

When she reached home she told Bert Pinnegar of fabulous morning glories, all blue, so blue, in fact, that once you had seen them you could never be happy again. For a countryman Bert Pinnegar acted promptly. He let it soak in for a week. Then, remembering a chance remark he had overheard on a previous occasion, he sat down and wrote to the Curator of Kew Gardens, who sent him a very nice letter in reply. The flower in question was the lovely *Ipomea Leari,* which grew luxuriantly in the open under sub-tropical conditions. Some writers, Farrer included, rated it above the gentian. During favorable English summers it had been known to blossom in the open air, but cultivation under glass was recommended. As Mr. Pinnegar appeared to be interested, the Curator enclosed a few seeds and hoped that satisfactory results would be obtained.

Bert Pinnegar planted the precious seeds in leaf mold, transferred the young plants into large pots, and, as they started to climb, let them run up to the roof through the branches of an old Marechal Neil rose, where they were well hidden from sight. Very soon, long pointed buds, like a folded umbrella, began to appear; and, one morning—the miracle happened.

Running up to the house, "for all the world as if the place was on fire," he left an urgent message at the back door for the housekeeper to send the missus along to the big greenhouse, so soon as she was up and about. The call, reaching Mrs. Charteris with her early cup of tea, was received with commendable composure. Having spent a luxurious half-hour in the bathroom, she completed her toilet; discussed with Mrs. Garlick certain household problems of no immediate importance; opened her letters, and, breakfast being cleared away, strolled across to the big greenhouse, prepared for any horticultural calamity that might have occurred during the night.

Bert Pinnegar was standing as he had been standing for the past hour, at the foot of the Marechal Neil rose. His Lady smiled at him graciously.

"Good morning, Pinnegar," she said. "Is anything the matter? Mrs. Garlick said you wanted to see me." Then she waited composedly for whatever tale of woe he might have to tell.

But the strain of waiting had been too great. He could find no words to fit the occasion. All he could do was to point mutely to the roof of the big greenhouse.

Mrs. Charteris raised her eyes, and, seeing the drift of blue blossom, gave a little cry of sheer happiness. Once again she felt that tug at the heart, a kind of suffocation that almost hurt. Once again she was drifting over a blue sea, under a blue sky, into a lovely land of blue nothingness. . . .

"Oh, Pinnegar," she said. "How kind of you—how very, very kind!"

CHAPTER ELEVEN

The Victorian Age, with its sound, smug and rather stuffy trappings, was succeeded by the brittle sophistications of the Edwardian era. Everyone was critical of everything that had gone before. Everyone had a better way of doing things. Those old men with long whiskers were six a penny. Why, even Dr. W. G. Grace was said to be a bit of an old chiseler. . . .

The sort of world, in fact, that did not suit Mr. Addis at all. So that everyone was a little relieved when he was swept up to heaven in a cloud of exasperation and Bert Pinnegar reigned in his stead.

Not that Mr. Pinnegar, as we must now call him, escaped the critical attitude of his younger contemporaries. Walking through the Manor gardens, with all his newly acquired honors thick upon him, he found young Jim Mustoe's prong lying athwart a grass path, where it had been placed with careful precision two minutes before. Young Mustoe and a couple of cronies were lurking behind a handy bush in the hope of taking a rise out of their new boss.

"Whose prong is this?" asked Mr. Pinnegar.

"Mine, Bert," replied the owner.

"Pick it up," ordered Mr. Pinnegar.

"Pick it up yourself," said young Mustoe.

It is never wise to force an issue unless you see your way clear to carry it through. The newly ordained head gardener had two alternatives—equally impossible. He couldn't hit young Mustoe on the nose, because, physically, young Mustoe was a bigger and better man. He couldn't report young Mustoe to Higher Authority, because that would have been an admission that he wasn't man enough to control his staff. Young Mustoe and his associates grinned happily.

Yet, oddly enough, Mr. Pinnegar didn't seem at all worried. Quite friendly, in fact. "Look here, Jim," he said. "Suppose, as well might be, you had just been made head gardener, and suppose some silly young devil told you to pick up his prong—what would you do?"

"I'd see him d—d first," said young Mustoe.

"Quite right, Jim," agreed the new head gardener, with an approving nod. "Right first time. If you go on like that, Jim, you'll be head gardener yourself, one of these fine days."

Dazzled by this prospect, young Mustoe stooped to pick up his prong; but his new guv'nor hadn't finished with him yet. "And, Jim," he added benevolently, "when you're head gardener, always see that the other fellows call you Mr. Mustoe; a bit difficult at first, Jim, but you'll find it pays in the long run."

"Yes, Mr. Pinnegar," replied young Mustoe.

Mr. Pinnegar wandered away, leaving the unholy trinity to pick the bones out of that one. He had won his first skirmish and, so far as his staff was concerned, there were no further battles to be fought.

But outside, in the village, he felt like a fish out of water. You can't suddenly become somebody without feeling a bit self-conscious about it. Like the wife of a worthy citizen who hears herself addressed as "My Lady" for the first time. Very pleasant, of course, to be singled out from your familiar circle, but a shade embarrassing, until you get used to it. Of course his old cronies went on calling him Bert, just as if nothing had happened; but to the rest of the village, from top to bottom, he had become Mr. Pinnegar, whether he liked it or not.

And promotion brought added responsibilities. At the Parish Meeting, when they were discussing whether the old stile into the cricket field was getting a bit dangerous, the Chairman turned to him suddenly and said, "Now, Mr. Pinnegar, we haven't heard from you yet." Actually this was a kindly attempt to draw him into the charmed circle of city fathers, but it put him in no end of a spin. "Come along, Mr. Pinnegar, you've been in the village as long as most of us. D'you think it's time we had the old stile down and put up something more in keeping with the times, or would you rather leave it as it is—as we've all known it for so many years?"

It was the first time Mr. Pinnegar had stood on his feet to address a public meeting, and only the more diffident of us can realize the awful solemnity of such a moment. But the chairman was looking at him from under those bushy eyebrows.

"Well, Major," said Mr. Pinnegar, "if so be as you

think something new is better than something old, there's something to be said for making a change; but, if so be as you like the old stile as she stands, I reckon she's good for a few years yet."

The Major was an artful old warrior, accustomed to letting the villagers do exactly what he considered was best for them. He hated the idea of doing away with the old stone stile and putting up a brick abomination in its place. "Well, gentlemen," he said, "you've heard what Mr. Pinnegar thinks, and I'm sure we all agree with him. He likes the old stile; we like the old stile; all those in favor—" After the meeting, Mr. Pinnegar, who really had a rather open mind on the subject, learned that he had won a resounding victory against fearful odds, thereby saving his native village from a contamination worse than all the plagues of Egypt rolled into one.

Having learned to swim by being thrown in at the deep end, as it were, Mr. Pinnegar quietly developed a natural talent for saying what he thought in the fewest possible words. Unlike the average gas-bag who is always ready to talk about anything, he stuck to his own subject, and very soon discovered that the best way to learn is to teach others who know a little less than you do. He gave short, homely talks in the village institute, and spent much of his spare time reading gardening books, until he came to be looked upon as something of an authority.

Mrs. Charteris followed the quiet development of her new head gardener with a good deal of interest, and not a little relief. The experiment—and it had been an experiment—was working out quite nicely. The gardens were looking better than ever, and neighbors from the other big houses were beginning to copy her improvements. Her only fear was that some unscrupulous newcomer might tempt Pinnegar away with a bigger salary than she could afford. She need not have worried. Mr. Pinnegar was not likely to forget the lovely, laughing lady of the flower show who had given him his first chance. He was her man, for ever—and a day. . . .

When you begin to move up in the world you find, to your surprise, that there are such things as wheels within wheels. You are in a position to help people who are in a position to help you. Little courtesies are exchanged which bring advantages to both parties. And, as two heads are always better than one, you find yourself traveling along the road to success at double the speed. City gentlemen refer to their opposite numbers as "very good friends of ours," and what obtains east of Ludgate Circus also holds good in the quiet backwaters of a country garden.

Mr. Pinnegar was taking a last look round the place one winter evening when he saw the local station-master coming towards him with a large parcel. Mr. Honey and he were old cronies in a manner of speaking. Once a week they played dominoes together, and their respective positions permitted an easy exchange of Christian names.

"Hullo, Bert!" said Mr. Honey.

"Hullo, George!" said Mr. Pinnegar.

"Nice place you've got here, Bert."

"Not so bad, George," admitted Mr. Pinnegar.

Mr. Honey dumped the parcel on the grass and dusted a trifle of mold from the sleeve of his official jacket. "Came in on the five-fifteen," he said. "Thought you might want to get it in first thing in the morning."

"You shouldn't have bothered, George," said Mr. Pinnegar. "I could have sent one of the lads along for it. No call for you to be lugging a great parcel like that half across the county."

"No trouble, Bert," countered Mr. Honey. "Nice bit of exercise. Besides, I wanted to have a word with you about something that's just cropped up. More in your line than mine. I'm only a station-master."

Mr. Pinnegar awaited further elucidation of these mysteries.

"Letter from Paddington," said Mr. Honey. "It seems that every station on the line has got to have a garden, just to brighten things up a bit—take passengers' attention off the late trains, I reckon."

"Nothing very new about that," said Mr. Pinnegar. "Why, George, they've been doing that for donkey's years. *And* on the Thames locks. Why, I've seen pictures in the *Illustrated London News* . . ."

Mr. Honey accepted the correction with quiet dignity. "I know that, Bert, as well as you do. The point is, they're enlarging the scheme to include everybody—give us all a chance, blast 'em. There's a list of prizes as long as your arm and a special message from the General Manager himself, hoping that every station, however small, will have a cut at it. Well, a nod's as good as a wink to a blind horse. That means I've got to get busy. So I've come to you, Bert."

"They'll be sending a sort of committee of inspection?" asked Mr. Pinnegar.

"They will!" groaned Mr. Honey. "All complete with black frock coats and top hats. Looking like a funeral—*my* funeral, if I don't look slippy."

"How long have you got?" asked Mr. Pinnegar.

"They start next spring and they work round the system," said Mr. Honey. "They're liable to descend on us any time between April and October—and, if they don't find roses blooming all over the blinking place, there'll be the devil to pay. Are you going to help us, Bert?"

Mr. Pinnegar was, as we know, a man of quiet decisions. He picked up the parcel, dropped it in the shed, and walked down to the station where, in the fading light, he surveyed the battle ground—very much as Wellington might have done on the eve of Waterloo. And, as he ran a practiced eye over the conglomeration of lamp-posts, barrows and water-butts, he spoke words of comfort to the unhappy station-master.

"Listen, George," he said. "You can't do a thing this side, except keep the platform as tidy as you know how. You've got to stick to that bank, and a lot depends on when this precious committee of inspection turns up. Now, as I see it, George, they'll work along the main lines and leave you to the last. That means you'll be getting them right at the end of the season. October! That's your target, George. Now, what's going to make a show in October?"

Mr. Honey could have told him how late the five-thirty might be due to arrive, but that was about all. So he, very wisely, said nothing.

"Michaelmas daisies, George. That's what you've got to stick to. A real, good, whacking show of Michaelmas daisies. We shall be breaking up the borders next week, and throwing away tons of the stuff. Enough to cover a mountain. Glad of somewhere to dump it. Now you get your chap to dig over that bank and I'll send across a couple of cartloads—after dark. No need to let everybody know what we're up to. I'll tell my boys you've given us permission to chuck it around where it won't be in your way, and you can pop it in overnight. How's that, George?"

Mr. Honey asked what would happen if the committee started on the branch lines and worked backward, as you might say; but Mr. Pinnegar reassured him. Such action would be like going against the clock; almost against nature. People always started with what was under their nose. It was a gamble, but a gamble that was worth taking. Leave it at that. The stuff would be along on Wednesday, soon after six. How about a game of dominoes?

It all worked out as Mr. Pinnegar had planned. Spring had passed. . . . Summer had mellowed into golden autumn. . . . Harvest had been safely gathered in. . . . Mr. Honey was beginning to fear that he had had all that digging for nothing when, out of the eleven-thirty stepped three very important people. A little surfeited, perhaps, with their extended survey of station-masters' gardens; but quite prepared to enjoy the sunshine of a fine October day.

Mr. Honey spotted them at once, and sent his assistant haring across country to advise Mr. Pinnegar that the hour had struck. So that, before introductions were completed, the head gardener of the Manor had happened to join the friendly group.

Acting on instructions, Mr. Honey had not rushed at his visitors like a bull at a gate. He left them to do all the talking, and seemed faintly surprised when they brought the conversation round to the subject of gardens.

Most of his time, it seemed, was taken up by railway routine. Of course he liked to see the place looking a bit ship-shape, as you might say; but there wasn't much time left for gardening when everything had been seen to. . . . Mr. Pinnegar, now—there was a gardener.

Mr. Pinnegar waved such flattery aside. Anything he knew about gardening he had learned from his old friend, George Honey. Now, there *was* a gardener. If they doubted him, let them look at those Michaelmas daisies. Nothing to touch them on the whole countryside. But then, George always had swept the board with his Michaelmas daisies. What a show he'd had last year. . . . At which point Mr. Pinnegar gave the horrified Mr. Honey a playful tap on the ankle that lamed him for the rest of the week.

The gentlemen from Paddington were duly impressed. Certainly they had never seen such a show of Michaelmas daisies in all their three lives added together. And when you remembered that it was all done after office hours, for the sheer love of the thing. . . . Mr. Pinnegar gave Mr. Honey another tap on his sore ankle, and wandered away into that vague countryside from which he had so fortuitously appeared.

Three months later it became known that the first prize for the best railway garden in the Western Area had been awarded to Mr. George Honey, late station-master at Fairfield—recently promoted to Swancombe Junction.

And even that is not quite the end of the story. On a cold morning in March, a party of professional gardeners drawn from all over the county are standing on the up-platform of Swancombe Junction, waiting for the London train to take them to a conference of county delegates. Suddenly, out of the cold mist appears a glorious figure in a handsome uniform, trimmed with gold braid. The station-master, for it is none other, approaches the youngest and least distinguished of this distinguished group. "Why, Mr. Pinnegar," he exclaims, "well, this *is* a pleasure. Now, if you and your friends will stay just where you are till the train comes in, we'll see you're made comfortable. Don't often see you this way, Mr. Pinnegar. Quite neglected us, you have. . . . Ah, here she comes!"

The London train came slowly to rest, and the bewildered gardeners received the sort of treatment reserved for royalty. If there had been time George Honey would have had the red carpet out, but, failing that, he did all the next best things. A first class carriage, half a dozen foot-warmers, instructions to the guard that these were no ordinary travelers, and, greatest compliment of all, the station-master standing on the footboard to wish them a last god-speed as the train moved out of the station. . . .

"My word, Mr. Pinnegar," said the leader of the party, "you seem to be well known in these parts. They couldn't have made more fuss of you, not if you'd been the Lord Mayor of London."

But Mr. Pinnegar said nothing. He was nursing an extremely sore ankle, which the station-master had given a playful tap during his bit of friendly play-acting.

George Honey, like the elephant, never forgot.

CHAPTER TWELVE

When you have nothing to do but sit and remember, there isn't much escapes you. Yet, every now and again, Old Herbaceous would find himself forgetting some of the most important bits.

For instance, he would be telling them about Mrs. Charteris: what color her hair was and how she laughed out of the corners of her eyes; when someone would say: "But, surely she was married? What was her husband doing all this time?" And he would realize that he had forgotten to remember Captain Charteris; probably because he didn't often come into the garden.

Captain Charteris had been mad on horses, spent most of his time in the stables, and was killed at a point-to-point meeting over in the Duke's country. His wife had been standing in the Judges' wagon when it happened. . . .

"Poor woman," they would say, "losing her husband like that. Wasn't she terribly upset?" And Old Herbaceous, now remembering those dreadful weeks, would reply testily that "it would have been odd if she hadn't been." After which he would shut up like a rusty old jack knife—not because he lacked feeling for the unfortunate Captain, but because he had forgotten all about him and didn't like to admit it.

After all, that was the best part of sixty years ago, and sixty years is a long time, whichever way you look at it. If a man had to remember everything that happened to everybody in sixty years, he'd have his work cut out. How would *they* like to be asked, sudden like, about someone who had been dead before most of them were born?

Nothing annoyed Old Herbaceous more than being *catechized*, and it was after some such tactless probing that he acquired the nickname which stuck to him for the rest of his days.

Said one old biddy to another, as she scuttled away from Mr. Pinnegar's cottage window: "Old 'Erbert be main acerbaceous this morning."

" 'Erbaceous! That 'ent a sickness of the body. That be to do wi' flowers surely: them as goes on for years and years, perpetual like, till you breaks 'em up and starts all over again."

"Time *he* was broke up," snorted the outraged victim. "Never see such a 'erbaceous old varmint, not in all my born days."

Old Herbaceous—and it is too soon to be calling him that—might let his mind slip, like the smooth cogs of a worn wheel, but there was one date he never forgot. That was the day in 1913 when the great Spring Flower Show was moved from the Temple Gardens to Chelsea. Mrs. Charteris wanted to see the show in its new setting, and she thought it would be as well if her head gardener had a little treat at the same time. They could walk quietly round the exhibits, order one or two of the new labor-saving devices, and discuss plans for the coming season. Arriving at Paddington in good order, they traveled round on the Inner Circle to Sloane Square and reached the Hospital grounds well ahead of the afternoon crowds.

Mr. Pinnegar expected something out of the ordinary, but, like the Queen of Sheba, the half had not been told him. The exhibits were, of course, wonderful, but what took his eye was the way owners of great estates and their head gardeners strolled through the big marquees, chatting together, very much as he and George Honey might have done at their own local flower show. It was difficult sometimes to tell them apart, for what with the employers wearing rough country tweeds and their gardeners being in Sunday best for the occasion, you were often left wondering which was master and which was man.

While Mrs. Charteris was resting on a rustic seat, for which she had placed an order, Mr. Pinnegar followed such a couple in order to study this social phenomenon. The head gardener, he noticed, always kept half a pace behind his employer. When they stopped to consider an exhibit, the latter did all the talking, but his head gardener was always at hand, with a metaphorical boat-hook, to pull him ashore if he got into deep waters. Tact, decided Mr. Pinnegar, was the saving grace on such occasions. You had to let your guv'nor think he was deciding what to order, while making sure that he didn't waste *his* money and *your* time. No use in cluttering up the garden with fancy things that would die on you in a week. . . .

They reached a stand on which every known variety

of rhododendron was displayed. A discreet salesman waited with an open order book to receive instructions.

"Yes," said the master. "I think we'd better have some of those. What d'you think, Perkins? Make a fine show in that corner by the summer house—what?"

"Very fine; very fine indeed, Sir John. If you think they'd *do* in our soil. We're a bit on the wet side—as you reminded me, Sir John, when I wanted to plant that magnolia. . . ."

Sir John rubbed his chin thoughtfully, as one pondering great decisions. "Ah, yes, the soil! Ours is a bit tricky for rhododendrons, eh, Perkins?"

"And the lime; *that's* our trouble," the head gardener confided to the salesman. "You can't go against lime. Wonderful for irises but, as Sir John says, a bit tricky for rhododendrons."

After half an hour of similar experiences, Mr. Pinnegar returned to his employer, dozing comfortably upon her rustic seat. Mrs. Charteris did not know, and Mr. Pinnegar did not tell her, that all her troubles were over; henceforth she had nothing to fear. Whatever foolish decisions she might be tempted to make, there, half a pace behind her, would be her head gardener, ever on the alert to see that she did not waste *her* money or *his* time. . . .

There are moments in the lives of all great men, when inspiration comes on the heels of some apparently trifling occurrence. A chord of music, a sunset, the smell of a beanfield after rain—all have played their parts in the development of latent genius, since the birth of Time. And, when you come to think of it, the world began in a garden. . . .

It was a very different Mr. Pinnegar who passed his Lady through the "Exit" turnstiles of the Chelsea Show and landed her safely at Paddington a good hour ahead of time. Sitting in the opposite corner seat he brooded darkly upon his new responsibilities. It had never occurred to him before that a head gardener, like the giant in the fairy-tale, carried the weight of a world upon his shoulders. Now he knew that the wise employer depended utterly on the solid experience of his professional partner. In that exciting moment Mr. Pinnegar donned a new mantle of self-confidence, and it fitted him like a glove.

Sitting opposite his sleeping mistress as the express roared through Reading, he marveled that he could have been so blind. Why should you ask such a fragile, delicate little thing as Mrs. Charteris, to stand up to sudden frosts, prevailing winds and all the unexpected onslaughts of nature in the raw? How could you expect a mere woman to make those sudden decisions with which all gardeners were inevitably faced? Mr. Pinnegar thanked his lucky stars that his eyes had been opened before any serious damage had been done.

If Mrs. Charteris had realized what was passing in her head gardener's mind she would have had the surprise of her life. She was not asleep. Her closed eyes and relaxed attitude sprang from two causes: the impact of London pavements on tired feet, and a feeling that if there were worse things than death, a railway-carriage conversation with Mr. Pinnegar might be one of them. While her head gardener completed his mental program for her sheltered life, she was arranging a more effective schedule to cover his activities during the coming weeks.

And so they came quietly to rest at Swancombe Junction, where Mr. George Honey was waiting for them.

The next morning, bright and early, Mr. Pinnegar swept through the gardens like a *mistral* roaring down the Rhône Valley. Nothing like starting as you meant to go on. . . . A bit of gingering-up was good for everybody. . . . No more slacking around. Now that he had taken the reins into his own strong hands he would soon get the team moving. . . .

Meanwhile there was nothing like setting a good example. Time he had that bed ready for those begonias. Mr. Pinnegar took off his coat and was getting down to the job when his mistress walked across the diamond-spangled lawn.

"What are you doing, Pinnegar?" she asked.

"Getting ready for the begonias," replied Mr. Pinnegar.

"I'm not having begonias there this year," said Mrs. Charteris.

"No begonias?" Mr. Pinnegar could hardly believe his ears.

"No begonias!" confirmed Mrs. Charteris, as though telling the under-housemaid that there would be no more letters for the post, and that would be all, thank you.

"And what would you propose to be putting in their place?" asked Mr. Pinnegar, in what he considered his dangerous voice.

"I haven't decided," said Mrs. Charteris.

"They won't *do*," rumbled Mr. Pinnegar.

"What won't *do*?" asked his mistress.

Mr. Pinnegar shifted his ground. "We always *have* had begonias," he said.

"I know," agreed Mrs. Charteris. "But not this year."

"Of course, if you insist," grumbled Mr. Pinnegar.

"I do insist, Pinnegar," said Mrs. Charteris; and that was the end—for the time being—of a head gardener's dream of new worlds to conquer. He had failed; but, like Icarus, he had seen the sun. . . .

How Old Herbaceous used to chuckle over that bit of bother. It was all forgotten in a week, but it hadn't been funny at the time. Shook Mr. Pinnegar no end! He was almost chucking up his job for a day or two, but you can't be angry, not for long, in a garden. And Mrs. Charteris didn't make the mistake of rubbing it in. They very soon got back on to the old footing.

And then the war came and all the young chaps went and the two of them were left to make the best they could of a bad job. That was what pulled them together. No time for little squabbles—no sense in quarreling about the pattern of the curtains when the house is on fire. . . .

During this period Mr. Pinnegar—kept at home by Anno Domini and a game leg—was a tower of strength in local affairs. If this had been a history of England instead of the story of a garden there would have been a lot to write of those days; but in the village the quiet stream flowed on. Looking back across the tragedy of a second war, it seemed to Old Herbaceous that the thing had never happened at all. His mind slipped over it, and he was into the 1920's before he could look round. Everybody a little older; everything a little different, and yet no particular changes that he could put his finger on.

Mr. Pinnegar, now fifty, stood with his fellows, gathered round the new War Memorial, to honor their gallant dead. Then he walked slowly back to the garden, thinking of the young chaps who had gone. And, once again, he heard the beat

> Of those indomitable feet
> As, down the road that leads to Journey's End,
> Singing of Tipperary and a Lady Friend,
> Came unknown poets, and a tattered flag—
> Storming Valhalla with an old kit-bag. . . .

CHAPTER THIRTEEN

At fifty a man is so set in his habits that his neighbors know the best and the worst about him. They said of Mr. Pinnegar that he had "a fairish opinion of hisself," but allowed that his head was "screwed on better'n most"—a not unfriendly summing-up of a reserved and serious-minded member of their own class.

Mr. Pinnegar—if we may place him on the point of a pin and study his peculiarities for a moment—*was* intensely reserved, and serious-minded to the last degree; but when his neighbors reckoned "he had a fairish opinion of hisself," they were a little wide of the mark. For Mr. Pinnegar had a chip on his shoulder.

Like most self-educated men, he mistrusted his own judgment. If you have been taught out of a book you know that what you know is right. There it is in print. But when you have to pick up your bits of wisdom as you go along, how can you be sure? So the self-made man, when trying to convince others, is apt to bluster a bit—if only to convince himself.

So long as he stuck to his gardens he was as right as rain. You can't learn about gardens from books—not the practical side, anyway. You had to start as a boy, digging weeds from between stones with a broken dinner knife; scrubbing the pots and the greenhouse floors. Then you became, in turn, an improver, learning to dig and stoke; a journeyman, working on the borders; a charge hand, with other chaps under you; and, perhaps, a departmental foreman. That was where most of them stuck. Either they hadn't got the brains to remember the names of plants, or they were too lazy to put in a bit of work in the evenings, or the girls got hold of them and they were married before they could look round. In that case, they generally chucked up gardening and became policemen, because the pay was better and you got a pension at the end of it.

A bit of a Pilgrim's Progress, thought Old Herbaceous, as he looked back over that long, upward climb. Always somebody or something trying to trip you up or pull you back by the coat-tails. Jealous of you because you didn't throw away your chances the same way they did. Laughed at you behind your back because you didn't get tight on Saturday nights. Then, when they were going down the drain, they tried to make out it was your fault. Said you'd only got on by playing up to the gentry. And ended by trying to cadge the bit of money you'd put by to keep yourself off the parish. . . .

But we were considering Mr. Pinnegar at fifty: a prophet not without honor in his own country, and a bit beyond. A stern and just man; apt to be a little trying at times when he happened to get a bee in his bonnet, but highly esteemed, in spite of his little oddities. In politics a Conservative, with a sneaking regard for the fading pattern of Liberalism; he grew, as time went on, a little stiffer in the joints, when it came to bowing the knee before those strange new plutocrats who were beginning to buy up country estates after the first of the world wars. And so, without trimming his sails unduly, he steered a middle course, which made him acceptable to the more reasonable members of his rather bewildered generation.

When the old Major departed to fight on other battlefields, Mr. Pinnegar was the automatic choice for the chairmanship of the Parish Meeting. An important position. There were only two meetings a year, but in between you had to be keeping an eye on things; listening to complaints and settling urgent problems that wouldn't wait. Usually a bit of common sense put things right and people got in the habit of bringing to Mr. Pinnegar's back door those little troubles that neither the Vicar nor the Doctor could be expected to cure. . . .

One Sunday afternoon, when the woman who "did" for him had cleared away the dinner things, there was an urgent tap at the window and one of the maids announced that Mr. Pinnegar was wanted up at the House —immediate!

Such a summons, on Sunday afternoon of all times, was so unusual that Mr. Pinnegar feared the worst. As he pulled on his boots he questioned the maid as to possible disasters. Had she seen smoke coming from the greenhouses? She had not. Had those heifers got in again, stabbling all over the asparagus beds? She didn't think so. Mrs. Garlick had come in from the garden with the message and had told her to slip across to the cottage and have Mr. Pinnegar there inside of two minutes. More than that she did not know. Would Mr. Pinnegar get a move on, because it was her afternoon off and there was somebody waiting down the lane. . . .

At the house Mrs. Garlick was equally unhelpful. If he was so anxious to know what the mistress wanted to say to him, why didn't he ask her? He'd got a tongue in his head. She was on the lawn waiting! Had been for the last ten minutes. Mrs. Garlick also had her own ideas about Sunday afternoon, even though there was nobody waiting for her down the lane.

On the lawn Mrs. Charteris was talking to a strange gentleman. Walking across the soft turf Mr. Pinnegar was on them before they realized it, and he heard his mistress say: "Well, Harry, I would like you to give him the opportunity. He isn't what I should call 'showy,' but he knows his own mind and he isn't afraid to speak it." Then, seeing her head gardener, she added: "Pinnegar! This is Lord Gratton. He wants you to do something for him. I'll leave you together."

Once again Mr. Pinnegar had the feeling that he was being taught to swim by being thrown in at the deep end. He had seen lords on platforms, but this was the first time he had ever in all his life spoken to one. How did you address a lord? What did you talk to them about? Did you stand to attention with your thumbs behind the seams of your trousers, or what? Thank goodness this had happened on a Sunday when he had his best togs on. . . .

Then he realized that he was being spoken to: "I wish," said Lord Gratton, "that we could get our carnations to look like yours. How on earth d'you manage it? Keep a special eye on them yourself, I suppose?"

Mr. Pinnegar mumbled something about these being only the border variety. In the greenhouse, now. . . .

But Lord Gratton cut him short. "To tell you the truth, Pinnegar," he said, "I'm not so keen on all this forcing under glass. All very well for table decoration—the ladies like something a bit showy, but my idea of a good gardener is a man who comes out into the open, rolls up his shirt-sleeves and has a rough-and-tumble with nature. Anyhow, the two things are quite different—it's like comparing a skylark with one of those parrots at the Zoo. Don't you agree?"

Mr. Pinnegar did agree, from the bottom of his heart. Here was somebody you could talk to; somebody who knew what you were up against. But he knew his place. He wanted to say how much he agreed, but no words came.

"You must have some very good boys round you," suggested Lord Gratton. "I've never seen a garden in better shape."

Mr. Pinnegar admitted that he had some very good boys—some *very* good boys.

"Don't be too modest," said Lord Gratton. "When you get a good team, there's generally a very good skipper."

Mr. Pinnegar allowed that boys would be boys—you had to keep your eye on them.

"Young devils, aren't they?" laughed his lordship. And Mr. Pinnegar agreed that young devils they most certainly were, and would be to the end of time.

Then Lord Gratton, having taken stock of his companion, got suddenly down to tacks. He was President of the big combined County Show, and his committee had been looking round for someone to take charge of the horticultural section. The choice of his committee had fallen upon Mr. Pinnegar for two reasons. Being out of the immediate show area he would be able to take up a quite impartial attitude and, as everyone admitted, there wasn't another man in the county so capable of doing the job. "Now, Mr. Pinnegar, what about it? Are you going to help us?"

Mr. Pinnegar was flabbergasted. All his senses clamored against being saddled with this awful responsibility. Who was he, Bert Pinnegar, to sit in judgment on his fellows? All very well in the village, or at a local show, but to be stuck up on a pedestal and be stared at by half the county. . . .

"Sorry, M'Lord," said Mr. Pinnegar, "it can't be done."

"But why not?" asked his lordship.

"Can't spare the time, not possibly," replied Mr. Pinnegar hoarsely. "Too much to do at home."

Lord Gratton demolished *that* argument. He had spoken to Mrs. Charteris, who had very generously agreed to release her head gardener for the duration of the show. Besides, Mr. Pinnegar would have ample assistance. There would be junior judges to sort out the various classes and prepare a short list. All he would have to do would be to come in at the last minute and make the final selections. . . .

"Sorry, M'Lord," said Mr. Pinnegar. "I'd do anything to oblige your lordship, anything in reason, but it can't be done."

So spoke Mr. Pinnegar, yet somewhere at the back of his mind he caught a glimpse of a small boy hiding in a corner of the tent at his first flower show, watching those other Judges, serious men with serious whiskers, and vowing that he, too, one day. . . .

But it was too late to change his mind now. Lord Gratton was the old type of country gentleman whose feet were deep in the soil. He knew the rustic mind, its diffidence, its natural dignity; and he did not care to press his point too hard. "Very well, old chap," he said, "if that's how you feel about it, we'll let the matter drop."

"I'm truly sorry, M'Lord," groaned the unhappy gardener, "but you see how it is. . . . No offense, M'Lord . . . ?"

"Good heavens, my dear fellow, of course not. Very much obliged to you for showing me round. We'll find somebody. Don't give it another thought."

At this moment Mrs. Charteris hopped brightly into vision and considered the two conspirators.

"It's no good, Charlotte," said Lord Gratton. "He won't do it."

"Nonsense," said Mrs. Charteris. "Of course he'll do it. Now don't be silly, Pinnegar. It was very sensible of the committee to think of you; and very kind of Lord Gratton to come all the way on a Sunday to bring the invitation. I shall be very cross with you, Pinnegar, if you can't see how sensible and how kind everyone has been. How can Lord Gratton *possibly* go back to his committee with such a message? Really, Pinnegar! I never heard such a thing. . . . We'll drive over tomorrow, Harry, and you can give us our marching orders. . . ."

The two old friends wandered away down the broad path leaving Mr. Pinnegar to wonder what he really thought about it all. It had been a narrow squeak. If Mrs. Charteris hadn't come round the corner, just at the right minute, he would have missed the chance of a lifetime, and then what a fool he would have felt. . . .

The show was a tremendous success: fine weather, record entries, and exhibits of high quality. Everyone agreed that the Judges had done a difficult job in first-rate style; Mr. Pinnegar mixed easily with his professional colleagues, and entered the luncheon tent in great good humor—at peace with the world and all that was therein.

Funny, thought Mr. Pinnegar, how you let yourself be frightened by little things, just because you hadn't done them before. Here was he, having the time of his life; regular cock-of-the-walk, as you might say; and yet, only a few weeks ago he had been scared stiff of the whole idea. Sitting at the top table, swapping stories with a couple of other experts, he could hardly believe he had been such a fool as to very nearly turn down such a chance. Ah, well, you lived and you learned.

Lunching in a big marquee induces a spirit of well-being and genial complacency. The seats may be a little on the hard side, but the gay picnic spirit, to say nothing of the cold salmon, helps you to overlook such trifles. Also, there is just enough formality to put a spice into the proceedings. As Mr. Pinnegar leant back in his chair enjoying a most unaccustomed cigar, the voice of the toast-master crashed, like a glorious roll of drums: "My Lord Chairman—My Lords—Ladies and Gentlemen! Pray silence for—" That, decided Mr. Pinnegar, was the stuff to give the troops. The expert on his left, tickled by the pompous approach to post-prandial oratory, gave him a playful dig in the ribs. Mr. Pinnegar smiled happily.

Meanwhile the President was having a quiet word

with the toast-master, who, in turn, was moving towards Mr. Pinnegar. In his hand he carried a hastily scribbled note, which he placed quietly on the table. Mr. Pinnegar picked it up, put on his steel-rimmed spectacles, and read as follows: "You reply to the toast of the Judges. Keep it short. We're all getting a bit saddle-sore! Gratton."

Mr. Pinnegar's first impulse was to be sick; his second, to get under the table. What he actually did was to wave a protesting hand at the Chairman, who waved back, pledged his wretched victim in a glass of excellent port, and resumed his interrupted conversation with the lady on his left.

"My word!" said one of the experts, "you seem to be well in with the nobs!"

But Mr. Pinnegar was past such friendly flattery. He was learning that pride of place carries its responsibilities and that, too often, we have to sing for our suppers. At any moment now that dreadful man with the dreadful voice would be bawling his death sentence to the four winds of heaven. Stricken by sudden panic, he obeyed his first instinct to slip under the table . . . thought better of it . . . pretended he was only looking for his handkerchief . . . and prepared to meet his doom.

"My Lord Chairman—My Lords—Ladies and Gentlemen," sang the toast-master, "Pray silence for Mr. Herbert Pinnegar!"

Mr. Pinnegar placed his cigar carefully in his glass of port; rose heavily to his feet—and found himself standing in complete darkness, with a roaring sound in his ears; like a train rushing through a tunnel. . . . And then, ever so far away, out of the blackness, came a tiny spot of light which got bigger, and bigger, until it almost blinded him. . . . He was back in the big marquee, and everyone was clapping.

"My Lord Chairman, My Lords, Ladies and Gentlemen!" said Mr. Pinnegar. "When I see working gardeners, and owners of gardens, all mixed up together as we are today, it makes me think of a lot of lions lying down with a lot of lambs. I won't say which are the lions or which are the lambs. (*Laughter.*) Some people think we head gardeners spend our days bullying our employers; snapping their heads off when they want to pick a few flowers for the table, and so on. That may be true in some cases, but not in mine. I'm frightened to death of my Lady, and I don't care who knows it. (*Laughter.*) I won't say she knows more about flowers than I do (*laughter*) because that wouldn't be true (*more laughter*); but she knows what she wants, and I see that she gets it. (*Hear, Hear!*) I've worked forty years in the same garden, and we're just getting it into goodish shape. Give me another forty years and we'll have something to show you. Well, the Chairman tells me you're all getting a bit saddle-sore (*loud laughter*), so, thanking you kindly for the nice things you've said about us Judges, we'll let it go at that."

Mr. Pinnegar sat down. Once again the President leant forward and raised his glass in token of a job well done.

The following Friday evening Mr. Pinnegar opened his county paper to see what they had to say about him. "The toast of 'The Judges,'" he read, "was submitted in felicitous terms by Colonel Darington. Mr. Herbert Pinnegar made an appropriate reply."

CHAPTER FOURTEEN

If you could peel the years from a man's life, as you do the leaves from a globe artichoke, you would find him having his happiest time between the ages of fifty and sixty-five.

The awful anxieties of youth have resolved themselves—he no longer jumps at shadows . . . competitors are not treading upon his heels . . . achievement has not yet lost its glamour . . . ultimate success, glorious and satisfying, lies just round the corner. . . .

A golden, mellowing period which brings out all that is best in a man. Kindliness creeps in; cheerfulness spreads its warming rays; even a little humor. . . .

As he neared his sixties, Mr. Pinnegar began to relax a little, and it was said of him that he could "take a joke with the best of them." There was his story of the farmer who believed in setting his chaps a good example by working alongside them when there was a difficult job to be done. Well, the farmer started a gang on turnip hoeing, and, after breakfast, he went out to join them, leaving strict instructions for someone to come along in half an hour, at latest, with a message that he was wanted up at the house. Unfortunately the message got forgotten, and the poor farmer had to go on hoeing turnips all the morning. Nearly killed him, poor fellow!

Mr. Pinnegar also made great play with those members of his staff who "worked at half-cock" during the day but seemed wonderful active when digging their allotments in the evening. One of these happened to remark on the lateness of the season. "Yes," replied Mr. Pinnegar, "even the allotments are late this year."

And there was his little lecture to all new recruits on the deep subject of plantains: "You can poison them—they likes that. You can try to pull them up—they thrives on it. Or, you can ignore them. . . . If I catches any of you young chaps ignoring my plantains, he's for the high jump!"

Up to a point he welcomed the new labor-saving devices; but, as he grew older, he discovered a younger generation that didn't like work, and so became a little suspicious of all innovations. At the County Show he rather avoided the eager little groups gathered round some surprising new invention in the machinery section. He liked to see the edges of his lawns sliced clean and not nibbled at by some new-fangled mechanical contrivance.

Even flowers weren't quite what they were. He remembered the days before musk lost its scent. . . .

"What did it smell like?" asked one of the young chaps.

Now how could you describe a smell? Mr. Pinnegar reflected for a moment. "What did it smell like?" he repeated. "Why, musk, of course. What else should it smell like?"

Sometimes the young fellow would ask "why musk had stopped smelling like musk?" But Mr. Pinnegar had an answer. "If I told you that," he would say, "then we should both know." And he would walk away, chuckling to himself. . . .

He was always friendly to wild flowers. On the lower slopes of his limestone hills, Great Mulleins (verbascums) grew like weeds. They seeded everywhere, and, if you weren't careful they became a real nuisance. Most head gardeners declared war on these woolly interlopers, but Mr. Pinnegar always had an eye to an accidental effect. He noticed that mulleins had a knack of seeding themselves to the best advantage. They would spring up at the angle of a wall, and, if you left them alone you got a bit of height and color just where it was wanted.

But why leave them alone? Why not bring them into the garden officially?

One day Mr. Pinnegar stood on the terrace, like stout Cortez on a peak in Darien. "What's he up to now?" asked the young chaps, and searched their consciences for possible sins while their guv'nor surveyed the garden scene.

Having reached a conclusion Mr. Pinnegar took his spud and proceeded to cut out all the verbascums that didn't fit into his scheme. The others he left, and, in the second year their great yellow spikes began to glow like giant candlesticks in a cathedral. As you stood on the steps of the terrace you could almost see altar boys moving round dim aisles with lighted tapers. . . .

It had been a very dry summer, and the verbascums, being strongly indigenous to that soil, had survived the drought, and so become the glory of the garden. Mrs. Charteris was enchanted. It would, she felt, be a selfish thing not to share this loveliness with her neighbors. Calling her head gardener, she told him that she had decided to throw the gardens open to the public on the following Thursday. . . .

Mr. Pinnegar, a cautious man, averse to sudden decisions, was a little disturbed. A few personal invitations, perhaps; but to let a crowd of trippers come trampling over the borders, breaking down the shrubs and stealing the flowers, that was quite another matter. With all respect . . .

Mrs. Charteris, we must remember, was a little ahead of her times. Those were the days of high garden walls and closed iron gates. You could live in a village all your life and never see the garden of the big house. The splendid national movement for opening gardens in aid of district nurses had not yet developed to any extent. How the public would behave under such circumstances was a matter of conjecture. When Mr. Pinnegar stiffened a little and feared the worst, he was true to the prejudices of his day. With all respect . . . he ventured. . . .

But Mrs. Charteris had made up her mind, and, when her mind was made up the thing was as good as done. The gardens would be opened on Thursday, early closing day in the market town; invitations would be displayed in village post offices, shop windows and other public places; and Mr. Pinnegar would receive any guests who might put in an appearance.

But here Mr. Pinnegar really stuck his toes in the ground. With all respect, he felt it would be more seemly if the Lady of the house. . . .

"Nonsense, Pinnegar," said Mrs. Charteris. "You have done the work and you must take the credit. All you have to do is to move quietly round and answer any questions. Just be your nice, natural self, and tell me all about it afterwards. Now, run along and get the notices printed; we haven't too much time. . . ."

When Thursday came you might have supposed that all the world had been waiting to see the inside of the Manor gardens. Cars lined each side of the drive; farmers brought their families and the cottagers were present to the last child. Even stray travelers, attracted by the crowd, pulled up by the roadside and wandered through the grounds—just as though the place belonged to them.

A great day for Mr. Pinnegar. The sun shone and the yellow verbascums glowed in the sunshine. And how folk admired them, to be sure. Almost like a firework display it was.

"Who would have believed it, after all this drought!" exclaimed a head gardener—thinking of his own bare borders. "Just a lot of mulleins!" said another enviously. "Ah, but they've been *artful* with 'em," said a third; and as Mr. Pinnegar listened he shared the happiness of the true creative artist, when appreciation falls like warm rain on thirsty soil.

Glowing, like his verbascums, in the sunshine of popular approval, he suddenly felt a piece of paper being slipped into his hand, a piece of paper which, on quick inspection, proved to be a one pound Treasury note. Mr. Pinnegar, having passed the tipping stage, was about to return it when he received a quiet dig in the ribs and turned to find two complete strangers, a larky young naval type with what Mr. Pinnegar considered "a rather smart piece" hanging on his arm.

"Hullo, George," said the boy, "still the same as ever. This is Gladys, the girl friend. . . . Gladys, this is George—my aunt's head chap, aren't you, George!"

Mr. Pinnegar was about to explain that the young couple had come to the wrong house when he received another dig in the ribs which said, as plainly as words: "Play up, old man. No harm in a bit of fun. The Fleet's lit up—do your stuff!"

These, Mr. Pinnegar reflected, were those gate-crashers he had heard about. They turned up at parties where they weren't invited, and got away with it by sheer cheek. Only last Sunday he had read that a London hostess, a Duchess, had caught two of them at it and had sent them packing. Still, there was no harm in a bit of fun, and the Fleet was certainly lit up. Very well, two could play at that game—he would do his stuff.

"Listen, George!" said the young naval bloke, "I only met this lady two hours ago, straight off the ship, and she won't believe this is going to be my place when my aunt dies. . . . How *is* the old lady?"

"In excellent health, my lord," replied Mr. Pinnegar, "but, as your lordship knows, not so young as she was. How does your lordship think the garden is looking?"

"Oh, top-hole, George! Top-hole! In fact, between you and me and the yard-arm, George, I've decided to give you another quid a week, just to show my appreciation."

"Your lordship is too kind," said Mr. Pinnegar. "Would your lordship care to look over the greenhouses?

Perhaps the young lady would like a few carnations. . . ."

All would have been well if Gladys had been satisfied with carnations. But Gladys wasn't that sort of girl. Put her in a greenhouse and she knew what she wanted.

And what she wanted, like a child crying for the moon, was the finest of Mr. Pinnegar's prize orchids.

"You like 'em?" asked the sailor boy.

Gladys nodded. Gladys clasped her hands together. Gladys certainly liked orchids.

"They're yours!" declared her escort expansively. "Everything's yours. Pick where you like. Skin the bush!"

But this was too much for Mr. Pinnegar. "Oh, no, you don't!" he said. "You touch one of my orchids and out you go—on your ear!"

The heir to all that great estate looked pained. "George," he said, "you forget yourself. If it wasn't that you have a wife and seven children, George, I should sack you, on the spot. Understand, George, on the spot."

"If you touch one of my orchids," repeated Mr. Pinnegar, "I'll lay my belt across your backside till you holler." Mr. Pinnegar's vocabulary had improved with the years. But, in moments of great stress, he relapsed into the vulgar, or common, tongue. The budding Nelson looked at him solemnly.

"That settles it, George," he said. "You're sacked. Dismissed your ship. Kicked out of the service with—ignominy. I hate doing it, George, but you've brought it on yourself. I'll—I'll—report you to my aunt. . . ."

It happened at that moment that a lady of formidable proportions, a real old battleship, was bearing down upon them. Mr. Pinnegar saw his chance, and took it. "Very well," he said, "report me to your aunt—here she comes."

For the first time in its long and distinguished history the British Navy refused to give battle. It turned tail and ran. . . .

Mr. Pinnegar thought he had seen the last of his two gate-crashers, but he was wrong. Five minutes later, as he was moving quietly through the crowd admiring his shining verbascums, a rather furtive young gentleman in naval uniform touched his sleeve, drew him quietly aside and whispered:

"Excuse me, old boy, got to get back to Portsmouth, haven't got a bean. How about that little offering I popped in the plate a bit earlier on?"

Mr. Pinnegar pulled a pound note out of his pocket and, with some relief, handed it to this distressed sailor.

"You'll need all of it," he said, "if I'm any judge."

Gladys *was* a rather smart piece. . . .

CHAPTER FIFTEEN

Old Herbaceous reckoned he could remember most things, but when he looked back the years between the two wars had a habit of running into one another. Sometimes he would put on his steel-rimmed spectacles and peer at the inscription on a Challenge Bowl, won outright against all comers, to remind himself of a date that had slipped his memory. Or he would run his fingers through the first prize award cards, which traced, like footsteps in wet sand, his triumphal progress round the principal flower shows of Britain.

Down in the stables and cowsheds they nailed all their prize cards on the beams—first, second, third, and even highly commended. If Old Herbaceous had done that he would have had to live in a house as big as the Manor itself. Even his first prize cards, neatly stacked in a drawer of the old bureau, took up all the room he could spare. Lucky he had kept them; if only to convince these young fellows that they weren't the only clever people in the world.

When Old Herbaceous was challenged on a particular point, he would open the drawer in the old bureau and consult his filing cabinet. He would let them guess and wonder and speculate; and then he would give them the facts. Having judged at shows all over the country, he was almost a national figure in horticultural circles. Secretaries of shows would write to him, and once—at Southport—there had been an interview with him in the local paper. "The doyen of the prize ring," they had called him; and though he wasn't quite sure what that meant, he had cut out the notice and placed it carefully among his other trophies.

During those splendid years Mrs. Charteris had been as proud of her head gardener as he had been proud of himself. Together, they had worked and planned until the Manor garden had become one of the show places of the country. People came half across England—even from America. . . .

It was too good to last. For the second time in a quarter of a century Mr. Pinnegar woke to find that the bottom had fallen out of his little world. Once again Britain was at war, and a garden didn't matter any more—unless you thought of it as a place to grow cabbages—or as a hospital for broken hearts.

Everyone seemed to have grown old in a night. Most of the young people had gone; strange children from the big towns ran about the village street; lawns were left to look after themselves; parks were plowed up, and weeds grew everywhere. . . .

Of course it had all happened before, but Mr. Pinnegar, now nearing seventy, wasn't quite the man he had been twenty-five years ago. In those days he had taken on every job that was going—carried the village on his shoulders; even found it in his heart to laugh when they dug up the flowers and planted potatoes along the borders. But not this time. He began to feel a fierce resentment against everything and everybody mixed up in this mad endeavor to destroy the gracious pattern of the world he had known.

There were so many annoyances. Village boys, for instance, were bad enough left to themselves; but when they got artful young evacuees to give them new ideas and back them up in their mischief, there was no coping with them. Mr. Pinnegar had got the local urchins pretty well taped, but these small Londoners fairly made rings round him—there was no end to their devilments. Added to which, he wasn't so nippy on his feet, and his striking arm had lost something of its old cunning.

Mr. Pinnegar set and baited all the old traps. He ran barbed wire where it would hurt most and tarred the trunks of his apple trees. He even built a hide-out in an old elm—and nearly broke his neck climbing into it. Once he thought he had caught them but they had stretched a string across the path and he nearly broke his neck a second time.

He tried appeasement. Baskets of windfalls were sent to the homes of these dreadful children, but they turned up their noses at his maggoty "cookers" and came after his golden Blenheims worse than ever. Lord sakes, how they did punish those Blenheims! There wouldn't be a decent half-dozen left for the table at Christmas.

Then he remembered the old trick of turning a poacher into a gamekeeper, and offered one of the London boys a job in the garden. But it only lasted a week; the young devil was so impudent that Mr. Pinnegar couldn't put up with him. Always telling wonderful stories that had no sense in them. Said the lake in Battersea Park was full of crocodiles and that two of his brothers had been eaten alive. Seemed to think that life was just one long First of April. In the end Mr. Pinnegar didn't know whether he was standing on his head or his heels, and sent him packing.

Then there was the land girl. *She* was a bright spark, and no mistake! Always talking poetry and wanting to know how crocuses managed to have babies. Wore breeches, she did, and thought that if you planted parsnips upside down they would keep cleaner grown that way. Finally he pushed her across to the farm, and the last he heard of her she was trying to milk a young steer with the stirrup pump.

So that, what with one thing and what with another, Mr. Pinnegar had a rather thin time of it, until, at last, his temper got so frayed at the edges that it was hardly safe to speak to him.

One morning a lorry drove up and half a dozen youngish chaps, in rare holiday mood, began carrying off the light iron gates that led on to the terrace. Mr. Pinnegar knew all about salvage, and the need for collecting scrap, but there was reason in all things. These garden gates, with their delicate Italian tracery, had been brought home by his Lady when she was little more than a girl. They were so light that you could lift them with one hand. There wasn't enough metal in them to make a good-sized bucket.

Mr. Pinnegar saw red. What really hurt him was the spirit in which these young fellows were doing their job. His lovely gates meant no more to them than an old iron bedstead flung in a ditch. Great fun they were having; and enjoying it all the more because they felt they were top dogs for once.

But what rights had one old man against a war-time working party with the law on their side? Into the lorry, among the rusty pots and pans, went those lovely, useless examples of a southern craftsman's art, and he was left standing in the middle of the road shaking an impotent fist. . . .

So *that* was what England was coming to! Gardens had got to go. Of course they had. That was only sense. But suppose you started pulling up flowers, just to spite someone? That was playing the Germans' game: when they cut down all those young apple trees in the French orchards. No doubt those young fellows had been told to come back with a full lorry, but they weren't going about it in the right way—too pleased with themselves by half. Like someone working off an old grudge. And what had his mistress ever done to them that they should be feeling that way? Something wrong there, concluded Mr. Pinnegar, as he walked sadly across the weed-grown terrace. . . .

Mr. Pinnegar had never envied the rich their great possessions. Not that he was servile, and knew his place, as the saying goes, but simply because he couldn't be bothered with so much responsibility. If you had a big park you had to see to the boundary walls and pay a couple of men to keep the trees in order. And when you had done this you were expected to let the public walk through it, as though it was their own backyard. If you had ten gardeners they all had to be paid, and when they were ill it was up to you to look after them until they were about again.

Take Mrs. Charteris now. Here she was, as near eighty as made no difference, and the whole estate on her hands. When times were bad down went the rents, and when times were better *down* stayed the rents. Sometimes he wondered how the old landowners managed to carry on. No wonder so many of them were having to sell out to strangers from the big towns.

Old Herbaceous, as we must call him from now on, was beginning to get worried about Mrs. Charteris. She was getting so old and so frail that she couldn't do much more than stroll on the terrace when the sun was shining and the wind happened to be in the right quarter. They had bought her a bath-chair, and he would sometimes leave her sitting in it enjoying the bit of garden they had been able to keep going. Sometimes they would talk about the war, and how easily it might be stopped if people would only get together and learn to understand one another. Mrs. Charteris used to say that if we spent our spare time growing flowers instead of talking a lot of nonsense, the world would be a happier place. . . .

One day, coming from the greenhouses, he heard her call him, and was frightened out of his life to find her sitting there so quiet. She didn't answer when he spoke to her, and when she *did* come round she told him of a sort of dream, almost a vision, that had come to her. . . .

Mrs. Charteris, it seemed, had been sitting thinking about the war and how wicked it was that people had nothing better to do than drop bombs on one another, when, up in the sky, she saw a curious black speck coming towards her. She thought at first it was a skylark, but as it came nearer she saw that it was a parachute with a man hanging on the end of it.

The parachute went on falling until it was quite close, and she thought it would knock her out of her chair. Then it spread out all over her, like an enormous umbrella, until she found herself sitting in the middle of a huge tent, like the one at the Chelsea Show. The tent got bigger and bigger, until it covered the entire garden—and there was Mrs. Charteris, sitting in her bath-chair, with a young German airman perched at her feet.

By this time Mrs. Charteris had stopped being surprised at anything. It seemed the most natural thing that she should be sitting there alive, with a young Nazi who, for two pins, would have blown her sky-high. Neither did it seem odd that the vast parachute faded away on all sides, like a silver mist, cutting them off from everything. There they were, sitting together among the flowers of the Manor garden—alone in the world.

The young German was quite a gentleman. He spoke excellent English and, as Mrs. Charteris had been to school at Heidelberg when she was a girl, they got along famously. He told her he had baled out because of engine trouble and hoped he hadn't frightened her.

"Bless the boy, no," replied Mrs. Charteris. "People don't get frightened at my age. Where were you going when you—baled out? Birmingham! What were you going to do at Birmingham?"

The airman replied that he was going to drop a few bombs and then run for home.

"Dear me," said Mrs. Charteris, "what a dreadful young man. Aren't you ashamed of yourself? Why do you want to drop bombs on Birmingham? What have they done to you?"

The young Nazi told her that the British, being jealous of Germany, had started the war in order to destroy the Fatherland.

"Nonsense," said Mrs. Charteris. "Don't be so foolish, and don't listen to all the silly tales people tell you. Why should you want to kill a lot of people who have probably never seen a German in all their lives?"

The boy explained that he was acting under the orders of his Führer.

"A very unpleasant man," said Mrs. Charteris. "*Most* unpleasant. If I had him here I should tell him exactly what I thought of him. . . . Now, if you'll be a good boy and promise me never to do it again, you can wheel me round in my chair and I'll show you the garden. . . . Has your mother a garden? Do you help her with the watering when you are home on leave? How many gardeners has she? I have one—Pinnegar. He's quite old, you know; almost as old as I am . . . over seventy and getting a little past it . . . but you mustn't say I said so . . . he's rather touchy and I have to be very careful not to hurt his feelings.

"He's been with me since he was a little boy in corduroys, ever since I can remember . . . there's no one else left; no one at all . . . I wonder where he is. . . .

"Pinnegar! Where are you? *Pinnegar!*"

CHAPTER SIXTEEN

When Old Herbaceous, hearing a cry, hurried across from the greenhouse, Mrs. Charteris told him all the wonderful things that had happened. He listened to the strange rigmarole of German airmen and parachutes that covered the garden, and decided that the sooner he got his mistress back into the house the better. Of course it might have been just a nightmare, brought on by the war, but even now she was awake she seemed to be a bit funny. Said she had given the young man from Berlin a piece of her mind, and he had agreed with her that if gardeners could only get together and talk things over among themselves, there would be no more trouble in the world.

Mrs. Charteris was very old and very tired, but, as the doctor said, there was nothing really wrong with her. Just a bit of war strain. Old people got like that. One of his patients had the feeling that someone was always listening to her conversation, which annoyed her intensely. Another was apt to mix up the present with the past, and talk to quite elderly folk as though they were children. While a third, a very kind old lady suddenly started behaving like an angry child. . . .

Doctors had all sorts of long names for such things; something to do with the frontal lobes; absence of inhibitions, and so on. But, speaking generally, it was just old age creeping on—and if old people started forgetting things, or imagining things, where was the harm in that? Lots of things were better forgotten, anyway!

Of course Mrs. Charteris couldn't go on running a big house—that would be nonsense. What she needed was a nice private suite in a nice private hotel on the south coast. Somewhere like Torquay would be just the thing; no trying winters, no servant problems, friends dropping in to see her—get rid of this rambling old place, which was no good to anybody. . . .

Meanwhile he warned everybody that their mistress might seem a little odd at times, give them a bit of her mind, perhaps, or talk to them as though they were still children. No more harm in that than a kitten running after its tail. And it wouldn't happen all the time. Just now and again, but they might as well be ready for it. Forewarned was forearmed.

And so it was settled. Strange young men, solicitors, valuers, auctioneers, made all the arrangements, and everything went like clockwork. In the village they said it would kill the old lady, dragging her half across England, but when it came to the point Mrs. Charteris seemed quite happy and excited about it all. Her only worry was the garden—and Pinnegar would look after that. Yes, she would have a nice long talk with Pinnegar. . . .

So the bath-chair was brought out again, carefully dusted, and Old Herbaceous wheeled his Lady round the garden for the last time.

It was a lovely May morning, dew on the grass, bees

buzzing round the hives and all the apple trees full of pink blossom. . . . Up in the big elm at the end of the park a cuckoo was calling. . . . Just one of those May mornings.

Mrs. Charteris waited until they reached the shelter of the old box hedge and then she told him to stop. "Now, Pinnegar," she said, pointing to the step of the bath-chair, "sit down and listen carefully. The Manor is going to be sold and I am going away. I should like to take you with me, Pinnegar, but that is quite out of the question; there would be nowhere for you to live and nothing for you to do. So I want you to stay here and keep an eye on the garden. You must try and like the new people. It may not be easy at first; they may have their own ideas of what is best; but in the end they are sure to come round to our way of thinking.

"Now, don't be *difficult*, Pinnegar. Listen to what they have to say and try to understand their point of view. If you find you can't get on with them you will have to leave; but I hope it won't come to that, because I want to feel that you are always here to look after everything.

"Now, Pinnegar, *don't* be difficult. Sometimes, when I ask you to do something you don't like you shut up like an oyster, and your face looks like a bowl of sour milk. I know you don't mean anything by it, but you can't do that with strangers, Pinnegar! After all, it will be their garden, and, however wrong we may think they are, we shall have to make the best of it. . . .

"Of course you can *advise* them and tell them what has happened before, but when you see they have made up their minds, give in gracefully and do everything you can to help them. And, Pinnegar, when they have to admit they were wrong, *don't rub it in*. That's a little failing of yours, Pinnegar, rubbing it in. Sometimes you look so virtuous that I could smack you. You don't actually say 'I told you so!' but you *look* it, and that's much worse. So don't do it, Pinnegar, or you'll be getting yourself in trouble and then I shall be sorry."

Old Herbaceous was a bit upset by all this talk of being difficult and rubbing it in, but then he remembered that his Lady wasn't quite herself and was probably imagining things again. So he kept his mouth shut, and Mrs. Charteris went on:

"You know, Pinnegar, people aren't really fond of someone else's garden. They pretend to be, and try to say all the right things, but you can always tell. . . . That's why I want you to stay here as long as you can and write to me sometimes, so that I know how you are getting on. . . .

"You have been very kind to me, Pinnegar, and I have always been fond of you—even when you were being a little difficult. I haven't forgotten the early strawberries —perhaps they will let you send me some every year— and the blue morning glories—they wouldn't travel, of course—but you must tell me when they are coming out, and I shall try to imagine them as they were that morning when you gave me such a nice surprise. And don't forget, Pinnegar; always be a good boy . . . do what Mr. Addis tells you . . . and learn a new Latin name *every* day. . . ."

Old Herbaceous looked at the sweet, tired face, and something came up into his throat, threatening to choke him. . . .

"Don't snivel, Pinnegar," said Mrs. Charteris. "Nice little boys don't snivel. Use your handkerchief!"

So Mrs. Charteris went to live at Torquay, and Old Herbaceous settled down to carry out the conditions of his trust. The trouble was that he wasn't so young himself. Mrs. Charteris might think she had settled the war single-handed, but it still went dragging on and none of the young chaps came back to lend him a hand. The place was beginning to look like a wilderness; the shrubbery was a jungle, and as for the grass. . . .

He got to hate grass in those days; you just couldn't cope with it. There was something about grass that made you think the devil himself had entered into it. When the farmers were grumbling about there being no keep for the cattle, the grass in the orchard would be high enough to cover the hen-coops. Sometimes the old man would stagger out with a scythe, as bent as himself, looking like Old Father Time trying to catch up with the calendar. Or he would take a billhook and go along the banks to give the daffodils and bluebells a chance. It made no difference. He was like King Canute—grass just flowed over him, like waves of the sea.

Sometimes, when the farmers were grumbling more than usual, he would offer them all the grass for nothing if they would cut it and take it away, but they only laughed at him. They hadn't the time, or the labor, to come nibbling about on a bit of lawn or round the roots of his apple trees. So the grass went on growing, always where it was least wanted, and Old Herbaceous cursed the day when God invented the stuff.

And then, of course, he had to keep an eye on all the

people who pretended that they wanted to buy the place. They came nosing round, asking silly questions and running everything down, as though they thought they would get it cheaper that way. Others would say how wonderful it all was—and that was the last you saw of them. He soon discovered that it is always the most unlikely person who buys the house in the end, and, being a straightforward sort of old chap, he resented being made a fool of. . . .

To be truthful, he wasn't so keen on selling the place. Of course he couldn't go on running the garden single-handed forever, but he had a sort of feeling that any change, when it came, was likely to be for the worse. Of all the people who had passed through his hands, there wasn't one he would have liked for a guv'nor. Perhaps working under a real lady like Mrs. Charteris all those years had spoiled him; or new times might have brought new manners. It was hard to say. And so, while the caretaker at the Manor did not actually cry down the goods he had to sell, he certainly made no outstanding effort to paint the lily or to gild the rose.

Not that he could have done a lot about it, however much he had been willing to try. If the garden was a wilderness, the house robbed of its furniture was like an empty tomb. He didn't go into it very often, but when he did it fairly gave him the creeps. Like a dead thing, all the life and scent gone out of it. Sometimes he would stand in the drawing-room and try to remember what it had been like in the old days. Odd that a carpet and a few chairs could make so much difference. Or was it because it wasn't lived in any more? Old Herbaceous had a queer notion that an empty house must feel rather sorry for itself—cold and lonely and forgotten. Like people did, sometimes. . . .

Every now and again a rumor would run through the village that the Manor had been sold. At one time it was going to be a school; but, after taking a lot of measurements, they decided that either it wasn't big enough or that the alterations would cost too much money. Another time the County Council was going to take it over as a sort of convalescent home. There was even talk of turning it into a country club and using the park as a miniature golf course. When people asked Old Herbaceous if there was any truth in such things he bit their heads off, and told them they would be better employed minding their own affairs. So that his reputation for being a cantankerous old gaffer grew, and flourished exceedingly, as the weeks went by.

Just when it seemed that nothing would ever happen again, everything began to happen at once. To begin with, the war came to an end. Old Herbaceous received a letter with the Torquay postmark, in which Mrs. Charteris "rubbed it in"—good and hard. Nobody had believed her when she told them about her talk with the young man from Berlin. They had thought it was only a dream, but now they knew better. What a pity people didn't stop quarreling and spend more time in their gardens. She hoped Pinnegar remembered everything she had told him, and was not being *difficult*. . . .

Old Herbaceous wasn't much of a churchgoer, and it came as a surprise to him when the new Vicar, a man with ideas and the courage to act on them, asked him to read the special lesson at the Thanksgiving Service. After refusing six times, he put on his best suit and his steel-rimmed spectacles—and thoroughly enjoyed himself. "For lo!" he read, "the winter is past, the rain is over and gone; the flowers appear on the earth; the time of the singing of birds is come, and the voice of the turtle is heard in our land." And, with the rest of the congregation, he recited, "The days of our age are three score years and ten; and though men be so strong that they come to four score years, yet is their strength then but labor and sorrow; so soon passeth it away, and we are gone."

He sat back in his pew with two problems on his mind. He didn't know what that bit about the turtle had to do with it, and he was rather disturbed about a man not being much good after he was three score and ten. Old Herbaceous was as near seventy-five as made no difference, but he felt as fit as ever. Not that he wanted to do a lot of stooping, or running about; but, now the war was over, there would be plenty of young chaps about the place and he would be the one to look after them, because he was up to all their little tricks. They would soon have the place straight again.

Coming out of the church someone stopped him to say that the Manor had been sold at last. It was the first he had heard about it, but he wasn't going to let on that he hadn't been told.

"A good thing for everybody," said the knowing one, who kept the village store and saw business coming his way.

"That's to be seen," replied the old man, with customary caution.

"Not a doubt of it," said the other, rubbing his hands,

as though he already heard the pennies falling into his till. "I hear they've got all the money in the world. Doesn't do to have a big house shut up too long. And they're young people, too. Old Mrs. Charteris was a bit past it. Now things will get moving again. Brighter times for all of us!"

But Old Herbaceous had lived long enough to mistrust those bright mornings. He liked a drop of nice rain before seven.

"Too gay! Too gay, by half!" he muttered, as he clumped back to his cottage.

CHAPTER SEVENTEEN

Very soon it became known that the Manor had been bought by a Colonel Widford who was with the Army of Occupation in Germany; Mrs. Widford was living with her parents in Scotland, and there would be no one in residence for quite a while yet. In their absence Old Herbaceous carried on in the garden single-handed—free to do all the work he could pack into a twelve-hour day.

One afternoon, when he was trying to separate the weeds from the hardy cyclamens, a strange man came wandering across the garden. "Hullo, grandfather," he said, "catching worms for a day's fishing?"

Mr. Pinnegar, who had been kneeling for rather a long time, rose carefully to his feet. "And who," he asked, "might *you* be, young fellow?"

"Not so much of the 'young fellow,'" replied the other. "Where's your guv'nor?"

"I've got so many guv'nors these days," said Mr. Pinnegar. "Which particular guv'nor might you be meaning?"

"Where's the head gardener?" asked the stranger.

Mr. Pinnegar was beginning to get a little nettled by

all this catechizing. "You've got eyes," he said. "Why don't you use them?"

"No need to be impudent," said the young fellow.

One of the inherent qualities of the elderly countryman is a tremendous dignity. You will come across it in the most unexpected places—in the stables, in the lambing pens, and, of course, in the gardens of the most remote districts. Only a very bold or very unwary individual will take liberties with these old aristocrats of the laboring class. Mr. Pinnegar said nothing, which, in any argument, is always a trump card.

The stranger was up against something he didn't quite understand. Looking at this ancient scarecrow, he began to feel that he had met more than his match. So he shifted his ground. "I don't want to stop you getting on with your job," he said, "but I've got to speak to someone in charge. Who is the head gardener?"

"I am," replied Mr. Pinnegar.

"Good God!" said the stranger.

"Anything so funny about that?" asked Mr. Pinnegar.

Colonel Widford's new agent, recently demobbed, with the acting rank of captain, thought it was the funniest thing he had heard for quite a time, but he didn't say so. Evidently the old boy had to be humored. "Been here long?" he asked.

"Sixty years," said Mr. Pinnegar.

"Good God!" said the younger man, for the second time in five minutes.

"And who might *you* be?" asked Mr. Pinnegar.

"Colonel Widford's new agent," was the reply.

"Agents!" said Mr. Pinnegar thoughtfully. "Agents! I don't hold with 'em. Not that I've ever worked under one, mind you, but I've heard a lot of talk, one way and another. A sort of go-between, I take it; neither one thing nor the other. Not quite master and not quite man. Plenty of talk, but no real authority. Sort of beggar on horseback. Not that I want to hurt your feelings, young fellow. . . ."

The new agent waved this aside. "Go on," he said. "I like it."

So Mr. Pinnegar went on: "Stands to reason," he said, "that if a master doesn't know enough about his job to run it himself, he should leave it alone altogether. When you get a third party coming in, it only muddles things up. Two's company and three's a crowd; that's what I always say. Now, look at it this way. You're the new agent —that means you're my boss, in a manner of speaking. And you know as much about gardening as our parson knows about ferrets. If you doubt me, just stand there and let me ask you one or two simple questions. . . ."

"Heaven forbid!" said the new agent.

"Ah!" said Mr. Pinnegar, "there you are! Called your bluff first time. *I've* got to do the work; *I've* got to do all the thinking and *you* go prancing up to the master, taking all the credit. Well, if he falls for that little game, he's not much of a master, if you ask me."

"I'll tell the Colonel how you feel about it," said the new agent.

"Of course," conceded Mr. Pinnegar, "if that's the way the master wants it to be, that's the way it will be done; but it looks to me like taking up a lot of time and spending a lot of money for nothing. If you're willing to learn, I'm willing enough to teach you; but it won't be done in a day. There's a lot to learn in a garden, but learn you must, for no man ever taught another how to do a job unless he could do it himself."

"I'll do my best," said the new agent, and drove back to his hotel, where he spent the afternoon trying to reconcile what he had been taught at the agricultural college with the more complicated pattern of his new job.

Old Herbaceous was no fool. He might have taken the wind out of the young fellow's sails, but the trouble wasn't over yet, not by a long chalk. If he could get hold of his proper guv'nor and talk to him as man to man, there might be some sense in it; but Colonel Widford was in Germany, likely to be there for months, and, until he got back, this young captain would be marching about, laying down the law, driving everybody crazy. . . .

Up till now he seemed to have been still working for Mrs. Charteris. The money came every week from the solicitors in a registered envelope, but now the place was sold he supposed all that would be changed. That meant he would be at the mercy of these new people and, until the Colonel came home this young agent would be able to do what he liked with him. Constantly threatened by some disaster, Old Herbaceous gave a jump every time he heard a gate click.

But the agent, having been once bitten was twice shy. He worked from a safe distance. As things got easier he would send a couple of chaps over from the estate department, but they always came with definite instructions and a specific job to do. Sometimes they were welcome and sometimes they weren't, but they obviously had orders to ignore the old man—and they ignored him, after the fashion of their kind. "What's happened to th' Old Age Pension, then?" asked one; to which the other replied, "Didn'st know, they only gets it up to ninety?" Then they both laughed, and Old Herbaceous knew that the golden days of authority were over. He could never deal with such unmannerly young cubs.

The delicate technique of persuading a man to sack himself because you were unable or unwilling to sack him is worth a moment's consideration. Different types call for different methods. You can nag him out of his job, by constantly finding fault with his work. You can lay an artful trap which prompts him to say, in an unguarded moment: "Well, if that's how you feel, perhaps I'd better go." Or you can humiliate him by ignoring the position he holds and dealing direct with his subordinates. Neither method has much to be said for it, but the last is perhaps the beastliest and deadliest—where a man of some natural dignity is concerned.

As time went on Old Herbaceous found himself isolated in a most peculiar fashion. Nobody took any notice of him. He would come in the morning, put on his old green apron, and get down to any job he thought needed doing. He would go home to his dinner, come back in the afternoon and work until it was dark; and not a soul would come near him even to pass the time of day. Every now and again strange gentlemen would walk round, talking earnestly among themselves, but for all the notice they took of him the old man might have been the stump of a dead tree. When they had gone other strange men would come taking measurements and almost pass their tape over him as he knelt by a border. But nobody bothered to speak to him. He might not have been there.

Mr. Pinnegar had never been treated like this, and he didn't understand it at all. When he was a youngster, everybody had some sort of a word for him; and when he was a real head gardener, he had a word for everybody. Not that you wanted to keep on chattering all the time. It was just common politeness. All this shuffling about, without saying anything, got on your nerves; and as for giving the young chaps orders over his head, that was just rank bad manners, and no other word for it.

Sometimes he would get hot under the collar and decide to find out exactly where he stood. Was he head gardener or wasn't he? Did they think he was earning his keep, or didn't they? Had he done something he didn't know of to upset everybody? What was it all about, anyway?

Full of some such vague resolution he would take off his old green apron and walk away in the direction of the estate office. And then his heart would fail him. It wasn't so much that he was afraid of losing his job as that he couldn't face life without his garden. Mr. Addis, or someone, had said that you got out of a garden what you put into it. How was he to throw everything away after sixty years, and what was he to do with himself if he did? It wasn't the money . . . there was enough in the old teapot on the mantelpiece to see him through—if they'd let him work for nothing. . . .

Then there was Mrs. Charteris, down at Torquay. He'd promised her to keep an eye on things. Well, perhaps that was stretching it a bit; the garden wouldn't suffer if he went, but it counted. When she heard that he had chucked up the job, and no reasons given, what would she think? Bound to be upset. Of course she would.

So things crawled miserably along until one day he

was told that he was wanted up at the estate office. The agent was sitting at a big desk and wasted no time. "Well, Pinnegar," he said briskly, "the sale has gone through at last, after all these months. Takes a lot of time, winding up a big estate like this; tenancies and so on, lawyers have to get their pickings, but everything is signed, sealed and settled. I thought you'd like to know."

"Very interesting," said Old Herbaceous. "Very interesting indeed." Now why had this busy young fellow brought him all the way up the hill to tell him that?

"What concerns you," continued the agent, with a shade less confidence, "is that we have engaged a head gardener. And you'll have to go. I'm sorry to spring this on you, as it were, but the place has been allowed to get into such a state of neglect that I had no option. There's a lot of planning to be done before the Colonel comes home, and we couldn't miss a day. Your own position is a trifle—nebulous, shall we say. As you probably know, you have been paid by the late owner, but now that the estate has definitely changed hands, any such arrangement naturally goes by the board. . . ."

"Mrs. Charteris always told me—" began Mr. Pinnegar, but the agent cut him short.

"The late owner," he said irritably, "certainly expressed the wish that you should be a sort of—ah—guardian angel—so long as you had the health and strength to act in such a capacity; but 'guardian angels' can be rather inconvenient things in a modern world, and Mrs. Charteris was not in quite the state of mind necessary to envisage present conditions. In a word, Pinnegar, I could only offer you a subordinate position under the new head gardener and, to be frank, I hope you will agree, as a sensible man, that this would be a most unsatisfactory compromise. It wouldn't work, Pinnegar—only trouble could come of it."

"Yes," said Old Herbaceous, under his breath, "you'd see to that."

Then the agent shot his final bolt. "There is, of course," he said, "the question of the cottage."

"Which cottage?" asked the old man.

"The cottage in which you are at present living," replied the agent. "We don't want to seem harsh in any way; you will be given reasonable time to find other accommodation; but that is a tied cottage and we shall need it for the new head gardener. He must have somewhere to live; somewhere near his work."

"Mrs. Charteris always told me—"

"Don't keep on bringing Mrs. Charteris into this," groaned the agent. "Mrs. Charteris has sold the estate, and she can't have it both ways. If she wanted it as a home of rest for tired retainers, she should have kept it. She can't have her cake and eat it. All this mixing up of sentiment and business makes everything so difficult. How can I get the estate in any sort of order if I'm met at every turn by the whimsies of an old woman who wasn't quite right in her head?"

Old Herbaceous pulled himself to his feet, and there was about him an air of strange dignity as he closed that rather awkward interview.

"Well, Mr. Agent," he said, "you've been very straightforward with me and I'm going to be very straightforward with you. What you say about the garden is true enough. It's been allowed to get into a state of neglect, and 'twill take a good man to make it half as good as it was. Good luck to him! And what you say about me is true, too. What sort of figure should *I* cut, doing odd jobs and running errands? So you can strike *me* off your list of troubles. As to the cottage, I'm not going to pretend that I'm happy about leaving it after all these years; but, if it's tied to the estate, there's nothing more to be said. All reasonable and above-board, Mr. Agent, except one thing. . . .

"You think my Lady was off her head because she found time, in the middle of all her own troubles, to think about an old chap who had worked for her for sixty years. That shows how little you know. There's still room for a bit of kindness in the world, and the next time you feel like taking a short cut across people's feelings when you want to get somewhere in a hurry, you might bear that in mind."

CHAPTER EIGHTEEN

Old Mr. Billiter, of Billiter, Billiter, & Billiter, had rather a weakness for elderly clients of his own generation. Handling their affairs made him feel young again. Also, they gave you better claret than the younger fry, who specialized in nauseating little drinks before meals and nauseating little drinks after meals, with nothing particular in between. As though you eat the two ends of a roly-poly pudding and threw the middle away.

"Give me," said old Mr. Billiter, "a man who knows what to drink with what, and which way to pass the port."

Every now and again—usually in the spring—old Mr. Billiter would toddle out of his little sanctum into the larger and more imposing office of his son, Mr. Harold, and begin muddling about among his papers. Recognizing the signs, Mr. Harold would call for *his* son, Mr. George, who, in turn, would press a buzzer for a particularly ancient clerk who was popularly supposed to have drawn up the original title deeds of Blenheim Palace.

"Griffin!" he would say, "the old boy's on the rampage again. What's cooking?" Griffin would reply that the affairs of old Sir Ralph Honeycomb were in a bit of a tangle—and the senior partner would spend happy days with the files and despatch cases of the famous Honeycomb clan.

This procedure, while it sounds a little casual for a big firm of city solicitors, had its points. Old Mr. Billiter had a prodigious memory and, in cases—or cellars—which interested him, needed no briefing whatsoever. He just dived in, like a dog at the seaside, and brought up the right pebble.

So that Mr. Harold, Mr. George and Griffin had handed over the documents relating to the sale of the Charteris estate with great relief, and no sort of apprehension whatsoever.

Old Mr. Billiter had spent happy months with those dusty records of an English family resident in the shires. It was like going through a packet of old love-letters—even though the ribbons were red tape and the scent was not exactly lavender. He remembered Charlotte Charteris very well; a charming young woman who had lost her husband under rather tragic circumstances, but had settled down, like a sensible girl, to run her estate. He had always liked Charlotte; indeed, at one time, when he had been going down there pretty often, it had been touch and go whether they wouldn't. . . .

At which point old Mr. Billiter shook his more sentimental memories aside and concentrated on the job in hand. For weeks he vetted possible purchasers as to their financial standing; wrangled with opposing legal forces and, finally, gave his blessing to the offer made by Colonel Widford, an excellent young fellow who knew a good horse, had won the D.S.O., and, greatest recommendation of all, was a member of his own club.

Old Mr. Billiter had studied all the aspects of the case with the most meticulous care. He knew all the details by heart and, when he passed them along for final endorsement, he did so with the comfortable feeling that Charlotte Charteris, bless her heart, had not been rooked by one of these smart young fellows who thought they knew everything but, thank God! didn't know as much as they thought they did.

In this flush of satisfaction, tinged with the rosy tints of ancient loyalties, it occurred to old Mr. Billiter to run down and settle any little details that might be outstanding. He could get there by twelve, have a bit of lunch, and be back in town for dinner. If Charlotte offered to put him up for the night, so much the better. They could have a chat about old times and there might still be a drop of that wonderful old brandy. . . .

When old Mr. Billiter got the scent of old brandy in his nose, there was no stopping him. Eleven o'clock next morning found him on the platform of Swancombe Junction, changing into the little one-horse train he remembered so well. At eleven forty-five he reached his destination. At twelve o'clock he was standing on the terrace of the Manor gardens.

The place was deserted. For the first time in his life old Mr. Billiter had forgotten something—his instructions to a local auctioneer some time previously to dispose of all that antique and modern furniture and effects. . . .

Old Mr. Billiter sat on the low wall and surveyed the desolate scene. The long journey from town had tired him a little; he was hungry and as baffled as a hound on a cold scent. That cozy little lunch with Charlotte was a mirage in a thirsty desert. That bottle of old brandy was as a dream that had flown.

Looking down into the neglected garden he saw a solitary figure approaching. Having wrestled with a rebellious rambler rose half the morning, Old Herbaceous was on his way home to lunch. Mr. Billiter hailed him, and the old man, unused to such courtesies, seemed doubtful whether to respond or no. Then he came across to where the stranger was sitting.

"What's your name?" asked Mr. Billiter.

"Pinnegar," replied the old man.

Mr. Billiter had a prodigious memory, and this rather odd name started it working overtime. "Good heavens," he said, "you're the chap who brought in those early strawberries the last time I was down here. How long ago was that?"

"Forty years, if it's a day," was the reply.

Old Mr. Billiter wanted to whistle, but he had somehow lost the trick of it.

"As long as that!" he said, half to himself. "Yes, I suppose it must be. And what have you been doing all these years?"

"Just muddling round," said Old Herbaceous. "Just muddling round. And a pretty good mess I seem to have made of it all. You would be the young solicitor from London?"

"We were all young once," said Mr. Billiter, passing reflective fingers through what were left of his gray hairs. "I remember you now. Mrs. Charteris wrote to me about you."

"Nothing but good, I hope?" asked the old man.

"Speaking from memory," said the lawyer carefully, "she implied that, with one exception—myself—you were about the only friend she had in the world."

"Very gracious, very gracious! Mrs. Charteris was a real lady. It was a pleasure to work for her, and I miss her sorely."

"Charming woman! Charming woman!" reflected Mr. Billiter.

"A real lady," repeated Mr. Pinnegar—and they, very properly, left it at that.

Mr. Billiter, having had nothing since an unusually early breakfast, was getting hungry. Indeed, he was in the mood to eat anything, as soon as possible. Where, he asked, could he find a decent hotel—and a cab to take him there.

Mr. Pinnegar had to laugh at that. The nearest hotel, apart from the little pub at the station, was nine miles away, and there were no such things as cabs in those parts. Mr. Billiter, a slave to the good things of life, was dismayed—and showed it. "Where do *you* eat?" he asked.

"Down at the cottage."

"Could you spare me a snack, just to keep me going?"

"There's nothing but a bite of bread and cheese, with an onion, maybe."

"I can think of nothing I'd like better," declared Mr. Billiter.

"Then you're kindly welcome," said Mr. Pinnegar.

At the cottage there was plenty of cheese, all the onions you could eat, and a bottle of beer to wash them down

When Mr. Billiter said it was the best meal he had enjoyed for years, he was speaking the truth.

"You've a nice little place here," he said, looking round the pleasant room. "Everything you want, eh?"

"I'm leaving it," said the old man.

"Leaving it? Why, isn't it good enough for an old chap like you?"

"Tied cottage," was the reply. "Wanted for the new man."

"But surely you didn't agree to that!"

Old Herbaceous gave a rather wry laugh. "Reckoned to end my days here," he said, "but you can't go against the law of the land."

"Law of the land be damned," exploded the solicitor. "Why, man, the cottage is yours—lock, stock and waterbutt. Mrs. Charteris only sold the place on the distinct understanding that you weren't to be disturbed. There's a special clause giving you a life interest; I drew it up myself. What the hell does Widford think he's doing?"

"The Colonel hasn't been near the place. He's still in Germany, all honor to him."

"Then who's been telling you this fairy-tale about tied cottages and—and all such nonsense? There must be an agent or someone in charge."

"Yes," replied the old man, "there's an agent, sure enough."

"Hasn't he read the conditions of sale?"

Old Herbaceous didn't know, but, in fairness to the young fellow, he suggested that things had been rushed a bit and there was a lot to be seen to.

"That be hanged for a tale!" said Mr. Billiter. "You can't play ducks and drakes with the law. Where *is* this young jack-in-office? I'll enjoy a little chat with him before my train goes. 'Rushed a bit . . . lot to be seen to,' indeed. Bless my soul. . . . Look here, Pinnegar; this is my card. If you have any more trouble write to me at that address. . . . Now I must be going."

If Mr. Billiter had suffered from high blood pressure, that would have been the end of him. The new agent certainly had it coming to him.

Old Herbaceous felt rather sorry for the young fellow when the titular head of Billiter, Billiter, & Billiter stormed out of his cottage and took the path to the estate office. What there transpired was never revealed, but the solicitor was driven to the station to catch the afternoon train, and it was a slightly chastened young gentleman who called at the cottage shortly after the office was closed.

In the excitement of the moment Mr. Billiter had omitted to mention his little meeting with Old Herbaceous, and so the agent was at a slight disadvantage when he started to give his version of the affair.

The lawyers, it seemed, had made a mistake. Although the estate had been sold to Colonel Widford in its entirety, there *was* a clause in the contract to the effect that Mr. Herbert Pinnegar should continue to occupy his cottage, as a life tenant, or for as long as he wished to exercise such option—if you ever heard such nonsense!

"I reckoned," said Mr. Pinnegar, "somebody had slipped up somewhere. However, all's well that ends well. Now we know where we stand."

"Obviously," said the agent, "owing to this stupid blunder, we shall have to consider the problem from a new angle."

"What problem?" asked Mr. Pinnegar.

"This question of the cottage," replied the agent. "We must try to hit upon some compromise, agreeable to everybody. Of course, we must have the cottage. We can't have a head gardener pushed away into some odd corner; he wouldn't stand for it; just walk out on us—and I shouldn't blame him. Besides, I've promised him this cottage. He's seen it, and the whole thing was as good as settled. Now, Mr. Pinnegar, as a reasonable man. . . ."

"But I'm not a reasonable man," said Mr. Pinnegar. "That's the trouble. I'm *difficult*. Ask Mrs. Charteris. Ask any of your young chaps. They'll tell you I'm just a contraptious old—"

The agent gave a rather watery smile at this little joke. "Yes, but, Mr. Pinnegar, you wouldn't force a technical advantage to such a ridiculous extent. Think of your position, living here right in the middle of the estate, knowing that everybody. . . ."

"What you're trying to say," chuckled Old Herbaceous, "is that you'd make it damned awkward for me."

The agent waved such an unworthy thought aside. "I'm thinking of Colonel Widford. You know what these gentry are. They like to have the place to themselves—monarchs of all they survey, and you can't blame them. After all, a man's home means something to him."

"Yes," said Mr. Pinnegar, "I was just thinking that same thing myself."

The agent tried again. "Mr. Pinnegar," he said, "I'll be frank with you. I'm in a very difficult position. When I read the conditions of sale I was a bit rushed and bothered; so much so, in fact, that I missed the clause giving you a life interest in this cottage. . . ."

"Ah," said Mr. Pinnegar, "I wondered when you were going to say that, and I think all the more of you for saying you were in the wrong. That being so—"

The agent leant forward eagerly.

"That being so," continued Mr. Pinnegar, "I'll pass on a bit of wisdom that was given me when *I* was a young chap. A gentleman who used to come down for the fishing said to me: 'Pinnegar,' he said, 'there's a catch in every contract. It's generally printed among the very small type. If you can't find it there, hold the paper up to the light. It may be in the water-mark.'"

The unhappy agent made one more attempt. "Mr. Pinnegar," he said, "I appeal to your better nature."

"Mr. Agent," replied the old man, "not so long ago you told me that business and sentiment didn't mix. Now you're saying just the opposite—swinging round like a weathercock. And a weathercock is only good to show which way the wind is blowing."

"Very well," said the other, "I've nothing more to say. You'll find this ridiculous clause won't hold good, not for a moment, in a court of law. You're no longer employed on the land. I shall appeal to the War Agricultural Committee. You'll be hearing from our solicitors."

"In that case," replied Mr. Pinnegar, "you'd better have the names of *my* lawyers—all of them. . . . Now, where's that card?"

And, putting on his steel-rimmed spectacles, he read: "Messrs. Billiter, Billiter, & Billiter, Leadenhall Street, London, E.C."

CHAPTER NINETEEN

After the interview in the estate office Old Herbaceous did not go back to the garden. Instead, he sat at his cottage window, watching the life of the village flow by, wondering how he was going to fill in his time for the rest of his days. If they were all going to be like this, he hoped there wouldn't be many of them.

The first thing he did was to send the registered envelope containing his weekly wage back to the solicitors. Mr. Billiter replied personally that it was a kind of pension, arranged by Mrs. Charteris, and would continue as long as he lived. . . . So he wouldn't starve. Well, that was a comfort, but the idea of getting money he hadn't properly earned worried him more than enough.

He hardly ever got out into the village. Somehow he felt that, in losing his position, he had lost everything that went with it. If he was no longer Mr. Pinnegar, head gardener at the Manor, who was he? Just another old man, fit only to sit on a doorstep in the sunshine, and talk about the weather.

He felt terribly lonely and out of everything. Sometimes he wondered why he had never married. These other old men had wives, younger than themselves, who bustled about the place, scrubbing floors, cooking meals, and, if the old men could be believed, leading their husbands every sort of a dog's life. That might be true, or it might not, but, when you were as old as he was, a bad wife was better than no wife at all.

Besides, if he had been married, there would have been boys—fine young chaps, who would have come along in the evenings and told him all the things that had happened during the day . . . and daughters . . . with, maybe, a baby or two. . . .

Old Herbaceous was reaping sadly where he had sown. All his life, all his love, had been given to a garden, and now the garden had let him down. Well, it was his own fault. No good crying over spilt milk. He must grin and bear it.

As Christmas came along he was feeling sorrier for himself than ever. All the other cottages were in a hubbub of excitement. Christmas trees were being cut from the hedges; shopping parties were being organized; everybody seemed more friendly with everybody. The only effect it had on the old man was that the woman who came in to "do" for him scrabbled through her work and was gone before you could look round.

No time, even, for a bit of gossip, though she *did* mention, just before she rushed off, that Colonel and Mrs. Widford were up at the Manor and that there would be a bit of a house-party for Christmas. Not that this interested him. It only made him think of the old days, when Mrs. Charteris would have them all in, one by one, wish them a Merry Christmas, and hand them the presents she had bought for them in London

Nothing like that in these days, decided Old Herbaceous. Most of that good old feeling had gone out of everything. What with taxation and rationing, people couldn't afford to be generous, and it was at Christmas that you missed such things most.

Thus brooding, the old man was suddenly roused by a bang on the door and a cheerful voice asking if there was anyone at home. Without waiting for an answer, the visitor, a rather jolly, middle-aged gentleman, marched into the sitting-room, announced himself as Colonel Widford, placed his shooting-stick in a corner, proceeded to make himself comfortable, and said:

"So *you're* the Mr. Pinnegar I've been hearing so much about." And then, as though something had struck him all of a sudden: "I've met you before. Didn't you come down years ago and judge for us at the county show?"

"You've got a good memory for faces," said the old man.

"It wasn't faces I was remembering. It was that crack of yours about all of us getting a bit saddle-sore on those hard chairs. And, by Jove, we were, too. But what I most remember was that you gave us first prize for a collection of vegetables—and how right you were! Don't say you've forgotten."

"I remember very well," Mr. Pinnegar assured him. "Never saw such parsnips, not in all my born days. You must have had a very good chap in charge of that kitchen garden."

"That's right, don't give me any of the credit," laughed the Colonel. "As a matter of fact, I wasn't much more than a boy, so I don't suppose I had much to do with it. But one remembers these things. We had a grand day and you gave us a good laugh."

Old Herbaceous was beginning to feel a bit uncomfortable. Very soon the Colonel would be hearing from his agent, if he hadn't heard already, about the trouble over the cottage. Then he might not feel so friendly. Well, no good ever came of covering things up. Better face it:

"I hope, Colonel, you didn't think me disobliging over the cottage."

"That's partly what I came to talk to you about," said Colonel Widford. "I met old Billiter at my club, and he told me something; then I met my agent, and *he* told me something, and putting two and two together, I'm afraid you've had a rather raw deal. Now then, what can we do to put matters right?"

"If you really need the cottage . . ." began Old Herbaceous.

"Oh, damn the cottage!" said the Colonel. "It isn't ours to begin with, and if it was you could have it, and welcome. What I've been wondering is, how an active old chap like you is going to fill in his time. You can't suddenly knock off everything without feeling a bit lost. Billiter says you're all right for money, but what do you do with yourself all day?"

"Nothing," said the old man.

"That's what I thought. Now, suppose we gave you the end greenhouse, to run in your own way, with no interference from anyone. Do what you like, grow what you like. We're very short-handed, and I should be glad to have it off my hands. If you happen to grow something a bit out of the ordinary, remember your old friends up at the house. My wife is always wanting table flowers—and she's got a *very* sweet tooth. So you can't go far wrong. What d'you say?"

"If your lady is at all partial to early strawberries. . . ."

"My dear fellow, if you put a plate of early strawberries in front of my wife, her eyes will pop out of her head like a—like a prawn! But you'll have to keep the greenhouse locked up, or you'll lose the lot. Here's the key. And, many thanks!"

Colonel Widford was half out of the room when he seemed to remember something. "Oh, by the way," he said, "I picked this up in town yesterday; if it's of any use you're more than welcome. Not that you need it, old chap. . . ." And he handed the old man the sort of shooting stick one sees in dreams. "You won't get saddle-sore on *that*," he said. "Merry Christmas!"

CHAPTER TWENTY

Sticky buds appeared on the chestnut trees, and little red tassels on the nut bushes. The aconites came and went. Village boys cut slides on what was left of the old canal. An early daffodil shivered in a corner of the orchard. But, down in the lower greenhouse Old Herbaceous was as snug as a squirrel in a hollow tree.

Every morning, whatever the weather, he would wander across from the cottage leaning on his wonderful shooting-stick. He never moved without it. It seemed to be a symbol of everything he had achieved . . . a hallmark . . . an outward and visible sign. So long as he had it with him he was everything he had ever been: he could look the world straight in the eye, feel he was as good as the next man.

It didn't hurt him any more to know that his garden was in other hands. Here, in the greenhouse, he was king of his own castle. Sometimes the new head gardener would drop in for a bit of advice. He would pretend to be worried about some valuable shrub, or bothered by some local condition that was new to him. What did Mr.

Pinnegar think? Was it safe to transplant, or had they better wait and see what happened?

Then, on very cold mornings, when their guv'nor didn't happen to be around, the young fellows would slip in to ask Mr. Pinnegar's advice on this and that—and to warm their fingers at the stove. The old man would send them packing, but it all made for good fellowship, and helped to pass the time. Even the Colonel would stop for a chat, and smile to find his little plan working out so well.

Altogether, taking one thing with another, it was the happiest time Old Herbaceous had ever known. They still smiled at him behind his back; but only as you might smile at the lines of some famous old battleship. And when they used his nickname, still behind his back, they thought less of the "acerbaceousness" that had prompted it, than of those wide borders where hardy perennials bloom newly with each succeeding summer and continue to do so for the life of a man.

About the middle of April Old Herbaceous appeared up at the house with the early strawberries that were to make Mrs. Widford's eyes pop out of her head. That lady, duly warned by her husband, rose nobly to the occasion, and the old man was made to feel that any little kindness he might have received had now been repaid a thousandfold. Once again he explained how important it was not to bring the plants into the greenhouse until the worst of the winter was over; how his late mistress had always looked for her early strawberries, and how he had promised to let her have some if the Colonel and his lady were agreeable.

After he had gone Colonel Widford and his wife exchanged glances. They were a happy couple who thought the same nice things at the same time. . . .

"How far is it to Torquay?" asked Mrs. Widford.

"Round about a hundred," replied her husband. "Not more than five hours' running time, there and back. Feel up to it?"

"Rather! Nothing I'd like better."

"Good for you! We'll start at ten; lunch; and have the old boy back in time for supper. Y'know, Eileen, you *do* get rather nice ideas sometimes. . . ."

"Oh, no, you don't," laughed Mrs. Widford. "If it kills him, you're to blame. I'll tell them to have something hot ready for him when we get home."

At ten o'clock the next morning, packed up with all the rugs and cushions in the world, Mr. Pinnegar sat, like a lord, in the back seat of the Rolls Royce, wondering what was happening to him. In his lap was a basket of early strawberries and, by his side, his beloved shooting-stick. Mrs. Widford, sitting next to her husband, carried a large bunch of violets—provided by Mr. Pinnegar. She turned and smiled at her passenger.

"Comfortable?" she asked.

The old man, finding no words to fit such a situation, gave a little sigh of satisfaction. "Home, John!" said Mrs. Widford, "and don't spare the horses." The big car slid quietly down the drive, turned into the main road, and headed for the west.

For the first thirty miles Old Herbaceous tried hard to believe that this wonderful thing had any basis in fact. Then he gave up the attempt and went to sleep among his cushions. When he woke they had stopped outside a pleasant little hotel on the sea front. Colonel Widford was speaking to the hall porter, who seemed to be expecting them.

"Mr. Pinnegar," said the Colonel, "has called to see Mrs. Charteris. I rang up last night to say he was coming. We shall call for him during the afternoon. Keep an eye on him, give him a good lunch, and, if he has finished before we're back, find him a warm corner somewhere. If there's a garden handy, let him have a look round—he'll tell you what's wrong with it. . . . Good-bye, old chap. See you later."

In the hotel the old man was handed over to a nice comfortable person. "Now, Mr. Pinnegar," she warned him, "you mustn't feel hurt if Mrs. Charteris doesn't seem to know you. Actually, she remembers you very well. She often talks of you; but you know how it is with very old people: one never can be quite sure what they are going to say, or what they are going to do. I won't come in; seeing two people at the same time might confuse her. You can leave your hat here. Don't let her talk too much, and you mustn't stay long. I'll come in and tell you when it's time to go."

The door was opened quietly and Mr. Pinnegar stepped into a beautiful room with wide windows looking over the sea. It was as full of sunshine as it could hold, and the delicate scent from a bowl of sweet violets came like the faint breath of a spring morning. His old mistress was sitting in a deep armchair, looking very much as when he had said good-bye to her in the garden.

"Good morning," said Mrs. Charteris. "I hear you want to see me. What can I do for you?"

Mr. Pinnegar produced his offering and placed it on the low table beside her.

"Strawberries—and so early!" exclaimed the old lady. "How do you manage to grow strawberries at this time of year? Of course, we used to have early strawberries at the Manor, but only because Pinnegar, my head gardener, was a very exceptional man. Very exceptional! He started with me when he was quite a little boy, and he never left, although quite a lot of people offered him more than I could afford to pay. I think he was rather fond of me, in his funny way. He's quite old now, but when he was younger there was no one like him, and the garden was really a picture. Did you ever see my garden?"

Mr. Pinnegar replied that he had seen it—many times.

"I'm glad," said the lady. "I like to meet people who remember my garden. Of course, it wasn't my garden, really. I was only the owner. I said that to Pinnegar once, and the poor man was quite worried; he thought I was being cross with him about something, but I wasn't. You couldn't be cross with Pinnegar, he was such a dear. Always giving me little surprises. Like a little boy who saves up his pennies and buys something for you at Christmas."

Mr. Pinnegar, a listener hearing nothing but good of himself, was becoming more and more embarrassed. He felt like someone looking through a window or listening at a keyhole. There seemed to be nothing he could do about it. But suppose Mrs. Charteris got to know she had been talking to him about himself, while he just sat there saying nothing. What would she think? Perhaps he ought to. . . .

At this point the door opened and the old lady turned eagerly to a new interest. "Oh, nurse," she said, "we've had such a nice talk about Pinnegar. When he came to me he was the funniest little boy. They wanted to make him work on a farm, and when I said young people should be allowed to make up their own minds the Vicar was quite cross. He asked me what I knew about the country, when I'd only been there two minutes." So, of course, *I* said: 'If it comes to that, Vicar, what do you know about the Garden of Eden? You were never there at all.'"

"You were very fond of Pinnegar, weren't you?" said the nurse.

"Not always," replied the old lady. "Sometimes, when he was being difficult, I could have *smacked* him."

"Oh, dear," smiled the nurse. "I hope you never did."

"Of course not. That was only my fun. But he *was* a little trying. One minute he would *exasperate* you, because he *would* do things *his* way, and then he would be so sweet you almost wanted to cry."

"How very odd."

"Odd? Not at all," said Mrs. Charteris. "Pinnegar was a gardener . . . just a gardener . . . and gardeners are all a little like that."